THE

MENTAL

GAME

THE

MENTAL

GAME

James E. Loehr, Ed.D.

Edited by Pam Stites

A PLUME BOOK

PLUME

Published by the Penguin Group
Penguin Books USA Inc., 375 Hudson Street, New York, New York 10014, U.S.A.
Penguin Books Ltd, 27 Wrights Lane, London W8 5TZ, England
Penguin Books Australia Ltd, Ringwood, Victoria, Australia
Penguin Books Canada Ltd, 2801 John Street, Markham, Ontario, Canada L3R 1B4
Penguin Books (N.Z.) Ltd., 182–190 Wairau Road, Auckland 10, New Zealand

Penguin Books Ltd., Registered Offices: Harmondsworth, Middlesex, England

Publiished by Plume, an imprint of New American Library, a division of Penguin
Books USA Inc. This is an authorized reprint of a hardcover edition published by
The Stephen Greene Press/Pelham Books.

First Plume Printing, February 1991
10 9 8 7 6 5 4 3

Library of Congress Cataloging-in-Publication Data

Loehr, James E.
    The mental game / James E. Loehr ; edited by Pam Stites.
        p.   cm.
    Reprint. Originally published: New York, N.Y., U.S.A. : S. Greene
Press, 1990.
    ISBN 0-452-26666-1
    1. Tennis—Psychological aspects. I. Stites, Pam. II. Title.
GV1002.9.P75L64   1991
796.342′01′9—dc2-   91-6490
                                                                        CIP

Printed in the United States of America

Original hardcover designed by Deborah Schneider

CONTENTS

FOREWORD

It has happened to all tennis players at one time during their careers. You're leading a match and feel confident about winning. Then, inexplicably, you lose it. Something happens on the court, you miss a few shots, become increasingly nervous and frustrated, and watch victory turn into defeat.

How did it happen? And why? And what could you have done to prevent such a disaster? And can you find the answers before it happens again? All of these questions have confronted players—hackers and touring pros; men and women; juniors and seniors; in singles and doubles.

As a journalist who has followed tennis closely for more than three decades, I have watched some of the world's best players squander leads of two-sets-to-love and lose in the fifth set, double-fault on match point, and tighten up so badly on passing shots that they could barely bring their racket to meet the ball.

As a player, I have also suffered some of the same indignities on the court when my forehand fell apart, or when my mind was somewhere else on a break point or an easy putaway volley.

Trying to overcome such embarrassments is easier said than done. But in recent years, much of my indecision as a player has been eased by periodic discussions with Dr. Jim Loehr, whose column "The Mental Game" has been a regular fixture in the pages of *World Tennis* magazine. Without question, Dr. Loehr has a better, more balanced grasp of the mental and psychological side of tennis than almost anyone. He has that ability to study a sensitive, potentially dangerous situation and produce logical explanations that can apply to every player.

It's difficult to assess the importance of the mental game in the overall framework of sports. In team sports such as football, basketball, baseball, and hockey, buzzwords like "momentum," "state of mind," and "the right chemistry" are often heard. Yet the presence of a coach as an authority figure and the overall impact of the team as a reference point often overshadow the role of the individual.

In figure skating, gymnastics, and diving, there is a premium on individual performance. Yet the effort is measured against a standard set by judges, opening another area of interpretation. In golf, the participant is generally aligned against a course—still another mental obstacle.

Tennis and boxing pit combatants against each other on a stage of their own. Both have elements that stress high levels of physical competency and dominance. But both also carry a supreme mental commitment. Boxers have often said that a title fight can be won or lost on the walk from the locker room to the ring; the same analogy may apply to tennis in the preparation for a match.

Some players believe that tennis is as much as 90 percent mental and 10 percent physical; others will downplay the mental impact, perhaps as a cushion against their own insecurities. But, as tennis extends its physical limits with more powerful rackets and the emphasis on stroke speed and topspin, mental strength becomes the tiebreaker in close encounters, especially among serious players and top professionals.

Dr. Loehr's columns are not simply how-to strategies based on his theories. He has counseled hundreds of athletes over the years, and many of their stories offer a real-life perspective that applies to everyone.

I can almost guarantee that after thoroughly reading this anthology, you will be a different person on the court. And your enjoyment of tennis will be a reflection of your mental satisfaction.

—Neil Amdur
Editor in Chief, *World Tennis*

INTRODUCTION

An old Chinese proverb states that those in search of the path to a treacherous summit should first study all possible routes, then ask someone who has been there. In tennis, only a select few have made the journey to the very top; their view is unique. Much can be learned from the study of great champions and from the coaches who helped them get there. The foundation of my own work in sports psychology began in 1976 with more than two years of interviews with top athletes and coaches. To this day, their insights and understanding continue to provide the basis for my work.

Two excellent examples of this kind of research are David Hemery's interviews with 63 champions from 22 sports as reported in his 1986 book *Sporting Excellence,* and the U.S. Tennis Association's survey of champions conducted by Ron Woods, Ph.D., in 1987.

Hemery has interviewed tennis greats Rod Laver, John Newcombe, Chris Evert, Billie Jean King, Margaret Court and other athletes, including Wayne Gretzky, Carl Lewis, Pete Rose, O. J. Simpson and Steve Ovett. The purpose of Hemery's investigative work was to identify common factors in excellence and achievement. Many of his findings have significance for tennis players. For example, the average age of specialization for champions was surprisingly high, at 16 years of age. Nearly all played more than one sport through their early teens. More than two-thirds reported being late physical developers and more than 50 percent reported being late emotional developers. In the area of family life, 98 percent of the athletes described their home life as stable and felt secure and happy as children. Ninety-five percent had parents who were not pushy about sports participation and 92 percent described their parents as being supportive.

Mentally, 100 percent felt emotional intensity plus control was a necessary and significant factor in their success. Eighty percent reported visualization to be a great asset to performance and 100 percent felt commitment and effort were the critical mental factors separating them from their less successful peers.

The USTA study revealed similar findings to those of Hemery's. Fifty-one American tennis champions (30 males and 21 females) completed a survey designed to profile the common personal characteristics, training practices, and personal developments of America's most accomplished players. The individual surveys were, in many ways, strikingly similar. The profile that emerged was that of a player beginning tennis between the ages of 6 and 10, while playing other sports as well, most likely basketball, baseball, or softball. Sole concentration on tennis did not typically occur until age 14.

Desire was consistently identified as the chief factor leading to competitive success. According to the survey, parents were perceived as playing the most significant role in the player's tennis development, followed by coaches. Personality characteristics considered most essential for competitive success were desire to win, confidence, good sportsmanship, and good concentration. According to those surveyed, success was attributed primarily to emotional and mental toughness.

In my work, I've found that professionals and casual players alike experience many of the same mental and emotional challenges while playing tennis. No matter who you are, there are four keys to developing mental toughness: building confidence and intensity; controlling nerves and stress; forming specific strategies for before, during, and after matches; and establishing productive goals and attitudes.

The following pages—a compilation of articles I've written for "The Mental Game" column in *World Tennis* magazine since 1984—will focus on these four crucial areas, with the goal of helping the tennis player understand the mental side of the game and learn how to use it to win. Reading about the problems faced by many players, from weekend player to ranked junior to pro, you'll see how mental-toughness training can help you win points, games, and matches—and shorten your journey toward fulfilling your potential.

THE

MENTAL

GAME

Chapter I

INTENSITY AND CONFIDENCE: YOUR KEYS TO MENTAL TOUGHNESS

Intensity. Players, coaches, and even fans talk about it all the time. From the sidelines, you can see when players have it and when they lose it. Anyone who knows anything about performance in sport knows it's very important to possess it, but has difficulty defining it precisely.

Intensity is energy activation. It is psychological and physiological arousal. The right balance of intensity leads to an optimum state of mental and physical readiness. In other words, you are in a position to play your best tennis.

Confidence. When you have it, you're different, very different. You're more relaxed and precise in your thinking. You move better, hit the ball better, solve problems better. You even walk differently, carry your head and shoulders differently. You're more aggressive, assertive, and attacking. You're less likely to get nervous. When you have it, it's almost as though you're a different person.

With confidence, you can reach truly amazing heights; without confidence, even the simplest accomplishments are beyond your grasp. I often wonder how such a simple human feeling has such a profound and dramatic impact on physical performance.

When you play tennis with intensity and confidence, you feel and appear unbeatable.

The Power of Intensity

If the dictionary defined the word intensity with the name of a tennis champion, who would it pick? My personal choice would be Jimmy Connors, because, over his 18-year career, he consistently dug down deep and gave it all he had, particularly when matches got tight. Nobody's ever called Connors a quitter, and no opponent can ever afford to count him out.

Bolstering Connors' intensity are his performance consistency—he plays at or near his competitive potential on a regular basis—and his emotion. He sustains a constructive emotional state when things go badly.

These three criteria—fight and determination; performance consistency; and a sense of fun, enjoyment, and challenge—can be used as benchmarks for determining a player's mental toughness. No one meets these criteria better than Connors, a model pro player whose style can teach players of all levels quite a lot.

Practice and play with great intensity.   This is really the Connors trademark, one of the keys to his greatness. Practicing for short periods of time at maximum intensity and giving nothing less than 100 percent during matches seem simple enough principles. But for many players, their practical application doesn't occur. Many practice with low intensity and then attempt to play matches with high intensity. Unfortunately for them, intensity control is a skill that must be practiced.

Use humor to break tension.   Over the years, Connors has learned to use humor to his advantage. A simple smile can cut the tension like a knife. Connors' ability to play with the audience, to poke fun at himself, relieves pressure. Humor can be a powerful weapon in breaking a stress cycle during match play. Humor often brings perspective, fun, and control to what could well have been an impossible situation. The rule of thumb is this: If you can maintain your sense of humor, you're in control.

When pressure mounts, get more aggressive.   Connors doesn't wait for things to happen when the pressure mounts. He makes them happen and goes for his shots. The normal response is to become conservative. The strategy of waiting for your opponent to make an unforced error is a dead-end street in the long run. When points or games become important, that's when you want to control your own destiny. Take command by being aggressive, by doing what you do best. It's percentage tennis, but aggressive tennis; if you lose the match, you've lost it courageously.

Love the battle.   Everyone loves to win, to the extent that most players can only enjoy the contest when they're winning. Nobody hates to lose more than Connors, but he's learned to enjoy the competition itself. And that's why Connors' love for the game never seems to die.

Master the challenge response.   Crisis and adversity are the real tests of mental toughness. We're all pretty tough when there are no problems. Connors' uniqueness lies in that he often plays his best when conditions are at their worst; rather than complaining or sulking, he just becomes challenged and digs in deeper.

The mental edge in sport is really the knowledge that when things get tough, you feel emotionally challenged, and that usually means your opponents will start backing off, playing poorly.

Project a great image.   Connors' on-court image makes a powerful statement about his character. His image projects confidence, energy, fight, determination, and control. Yet Connors experiences the same doubts, fears, and human emotions as the rest of us. The difference is he doesn't let his negative feelings and emotions dribble down his sleeve and onto the court. He appears on the outside the way he wants to feel on the inside; therefore, his opponents never see his insecurities and vulnerabilities.

Leave mistakes behind.   One of the most impressive qualities about Connors over the years has been his ability to walk away from big mistakes at crucial times. He's learned to let them go and get on with the match at hand. The inability to manage mistakes is the downfall of the majority of players. "I can't stand making stupid mistakes" is the common theme. A major part of Connors' greatness is his ability to "let it go," look ahead, and proceed positively when he makes a mistake.

Never run out of options.   Connors is a great problem-solver on court. If something doesn't work, he tries something else. Your goal is never to run out of options when you play. You're always probing for that weakness that will give you a new foothold, a creative answer to a stubborn problem. Do as Connors does: he never loses, he simply runs out of time before he solves the problem.

Lendl projects a powerful image of intensity and confidence. The message: look on the outside the way you want to feel inside.

Defining Your Terms

Although we know that our most enduring champions have it, exactly what is intensity and how can we consistently harness it and use it in our matches? Intensity is a condition of mental and physical arousal, of energy activation. Playing with great intensity is a matter of mobilizing your mind and body so that you are capable of producing your best response.

There are any number of things that can affect your intensity during play. Players have found that such seemingly unrelated things as amount of sleep, stability in their personal lives, current confidence levels, and how much competition they have had play a major role in performance. Other factors include poor fitness, diet, prematch preparation, and an overemphasis on winning.

Some states of intensity enhance performance; others undermine it. To become a mentally tough competitor, one must understand the difference. Intensity states can be grouped into one of four categories: high positive, high negative, low positive, and low negative. (Because intensity is so closely allied to our emotions, the four categories are divided according to positive versus negative emotion.)

You will perform your best when you can sustain a state of high-intensity energy that is fueled primarily from your positive emotions (high positive category). Feelings of enthusiasm, inspiration, determination, and challenge are central. You will best keep your muscles relaxed, remain calm, and concentrate when your intensity is from the high positive category.

High-intensity states stemming from negative emotions like anger, frustration, or fear (high negative category) often result in a variety of performance problems, including muscle tightness, frantic thinking, and poor concentration. Low-intensity states, whether from the positive or the negative category, foster spacey thinking, spotty concentration, indecisive and inappropriate shot selection, and slow and lethargic movement patterns.

Jimmy Connors is a prime example of high-positive and high-negative intensity. Throughout most of his career, Connors was quick to draw his intensity from negative emotions. At times he would literally toy with his negative emotions, producing inconsistency in his game. But, when Jimmy reached his late twenties, he began fueling his intensity with positive emotions, making him a tougher competitor than he was previously.

Martina Navratilova is another case in point. Years ago Navratilova's roller-coastering emotions left her prey to anger and self-criticism. But in the mid-1980s, when her high-intensity state stemmed from positive emotions, it was very difficult to break Martina's flow of positive intensity for even short periods of time.

Connors' and Navratilova's performance on court is ample proof that thinking and staying positive can only bring good results.

Taking Your Measure

How do you measure your own intensity level? Let your heart be your guide. In a real sense, heart rate (the number of beats per minute) is a window to our physiology and our emotions. Because heart rate is beginning to show promise as a barometer of intensity, an important question is: How does heart rate relate to performance outcome? Research indicates that there is a "zone of activation," an ideal performance state, that can be measured by one's heart rate. This varies depending on the sport and the individual. When heart rates fall below or above the ideal range, performance suffers.

Most of the research so far linking heart rate and performance has been done with sports requiring little movement, such as pistol shooting and archery. But I have worked with tennis players of all levels—from touring pros to club players—collecting heart-rate data. Here are some preliminary findings:

- Players tend to have an ideal intensity range as measured by heart rate. The ideal range is individual and varies with one's age and level of fitness.

- Performance levels tend to drop for most players when their heart rate at the start of the point is too high (above approximately 75 percent of their maximum heart rate) or too low (below approximately 55 percent of their maximum heart rate). You can estimate your maximum heart rate by simply subtracting your age from 220.

- Nervousness causes heart rate to increase dramatically (sometimes to over 200 beats per minute). Anger causes one's heart rate to increase unless one is already nervous or experiencing stress; in this case, anger causes one's heart rate to drop.

- Ideal heart rates for initiating serving tend to be lower than for returning.

- Drops in heart rate are often associated with winning a set, winning an important break point, etc. Such decreases in intensity often result in decreased performance.

MAINTAINING
YOUR INTENSITY

Here are some tips on how you can raise your intensity on the court:

- Attempt to trigger strong, positive emotion by thinking and visualizing things that are challenging and exciting (e.g., "I love to play the big points").

- Stimulate your feet by jumping up and down before service returns. Make a deliberate attempt to increase the speed of your first step to the ball. Prolong the point by keeping the ball in play, which will have the effect of raising your heart rate. By taking these actions, you'll work with physical movement to raise your emotional intensity.

- Increase your breathing rate. Clear your lungs by blowing out aggressively as if to blow out a candle. Be sure to breathe out fully and completely at contact point as this also has the effect of raising intensity. Grunting may not necessarily achieve these ends. It's the volume of air that's released at contact point that matters, and loud grunting often contributes to excessive muscle tension.

- Work to keep your eyes from wandering and keep your thoughts moving in a positive direction between points. What you do and think for that 70 to 80 percent of the total match time that you're not hitting balls has a tremendous impact on your intensity level.

- Develop the ability to courageously respond to adversity by investing more positive intensity in crisis situations. Our natural tendency is to either withdraw intensity or to allow it to become negative.

You can raise your intensity during practice, too:

- Generate more positive intensity in practice, both in drill work and practice. If you want to learn intensity control, you *must* create intensity in practice.

- Practice clearing your emotional computer quickly after making a mistake. This will substantially help to stabilize your overall intensity flow and keep it on the positive side.

- Set goals for yourself regarding intensity every time you play or practice. Rate yourself each day on how well you think you did.

- Use video to monitor intensity. Watch for two things: the number of intensity drops and the number of changes from positive to negative intensity.

How can you lower your intensity on the court?

- Slow everything down. Take the full 30 seconds between points, to get your heart rate down.

- Relax the muscles of your arms and hands by contracting and then releasing the muscle tension.

Jimmy Connors is "Mr. Intensity." He is one of the greatest competitors the game has ever known.

- Take at least one deep breath from your lower stomach before the next point begins. Exhale through the mouth with a long, continuous flow of air.

- Focus on simply doing the best you can, on having fun and enjoying yourself. When things get tough, smile. It lowers intensity.

The Confidence Connection

Confidence is the feeling that you can play well and win when you're supposed to. Unlike intensity, which can be fueled by positive or negative sources, true self-confidence is always a strong, positive, effective emotion.

Can confidence be linked in some important way to biochemical changes in the body? It sounds farfetched, but remember that confidence is nothing more than a specific state of mind. It has already been demonstrated that some feelings, such as nervousness, anger, and fear, have their own specific physiological and biochemical bases. In many ways, specific emotional states represent windows to our physiology, and confidence may be no different.

In a study conducted by a research team at the University of Nebraska in Lincoln, a possible link was discovered between a naturally occurring hormone called testosterone—which has previously been linked to assertive, aggressive behavior—and confidence. The experiment was conducted with the school's varsity men's tennis team. Specifically, the researchers hoped to establish a link between testosterone levels and winning and losing. Of particular interest was the question of whether decreases in testosterone contributed in some way to subsequent losses.

The study required that coach Henry McDermott's players provide a test-tube sample of saliva for lab analysis on the day before their matches, 15 minutes before, 15 minutes after, and 24 hours after. Players also filled out questionnaires before and after they competed describing confidence levels, expectations for winning, and performance evaluations.

Researchers found that testosterone levels did rise in anticipation of a match, but only slightly if a player thought his chances of winning weren't very good. Players who doubted their ability to do well had lower testosterone levels, and that translated into a competitive disadvantage. Also of interest was the finding that match winners produced more testosterone, but only when they thought they played at or above their usual level. The reverse was also true. Losers' testosterone levels decreased except when they felt they played better than normal. Testosterone levels actually went up in such cases, despite the loss.

The mind tends to follow the eyes. Andre Agassi's eye control leads to mental control.

Researchers also found that players coming off a win showed greater pre-match testosterone levels than those who had lost; testosterone level change persisted for as long as four days following the win or loss.

Obviously, the Nebraska study will need to be repeated and verified on a larger scale before the real significance of its findings can be determined. Regardless, as physical testing procedures become more sophisticated and reliable, it's likely that additional evidence will mount supporting this theory. Someday, science will verify what tennis players have known for a long time—that the feeling of confidence or its absence can produce profound physical changes in the body.

Controlling Your Confidence

The most important point for tennis players to understand is simply that to perform at your highest potential, you must learn to control your confidence. According to the Nebraska study, controlling confidence involves controlling critical physical factors necessary for success. But how can you control this elusive feeling? How can you control the expectation of success?

- Set the right kind of match goals. Confidence is directly tied to perceived success. The more consistent your diet of success, the more stable your confidence. The key is to set goals both in practice and matches that you can reasonably attain. The goals you set actually dictate your diet of success or failure; if you set goals over which you have little control, you lose control of your confidence. Basing your confidence on factors beyond your control is like playing psychological Russian roulette.

- Set performance rather than outcome goals. Performance goals are controllable, outcome goals are not. Typical outcome goals are to win the tournament; win the match; get to the quarterfinals; never have a bad loss. Typical performance goals are to give 100-percent effort; have a great attitude; look strong and confident during tough times; attack on short balls; play mostly cross-court ground strokes and down-the-line approaches.

- Set realistic rather than unrealistic goals. Don't confuse who you really are with whom you wish to be. Just because you once won a tournament or beat someone important doesn't mean it should now be your marker for success. Unrealistic goals eventually lead to shattered confidence.

Yannick Noah has got the look—confidence, fight, determination.

- Set specific rather than general goals. To do the best you can is an example of a general performance goal. The problem with this goal is its vagueness. The more specific and quantifiable your performance goals, the better. Here are some examples: get to every ball in practice before it bounces twice; have a first-serve percentage of at least 70 percent for this match; take a minimum of 16 to 18 seconds between points; hit at least four cross-courts for every down-the-line shot during baseline rallies; employ only positive self-talk during the first 20 minutes of practice today.

- Make short-term goals more important than long-term. While long-term goals are important, the short-term ones provide the success opportunities to keep you moving forward. Short-term objectives bring immediate focus and direction to your efforts.

- Find success in your losses. If losing is equated with failure, the battle of confidence cannot be won. Your motto should always be, "Win or lose, another step forward." You can find success in a losing effort when you establish clear performance goals prior to the match. You have the potential to learn much more from a loss than a victory. When you set your goals properly, your confidence can continue to grow, independent of your match's outcome.

Think Small, Play Big

Confidence is primarily an attitude. If you're confident, you look a problem straight in the eye and figure out how to make a positive out of a potentially negative situation.

Staying confident when you have a physical disadvantage such as size or strength is a predicament most people associate with sports like football, basketball, or wrestling. But it can apply to tennis, too. John, for instance, is a 15-year-old with a "small-person complex." Simply stated, John thinks he's too small to win. His opponents, it seems, are always stronger, taller, have a longer reach, hit the ball harder, and serve bigger.

At 5 feet 2 inches tall and weighing in at 115 pounds, John looks 12 or 13—at most. "I've always been too small to play tennis in my age group," he says. "I also have a bad birthday, which makes it even worse. Because I was born on November 27, on top of being super small for my age, I lose 11 months compared to kids with lucky birthdays."

As he continues to talk, John's anger and frustration mount. "It's not fair! There is nothing I can do to grow faster. If I had the size, I would beat the top players in my age group because I'm the better player. I just get overpowered. Everyone attacks my serve because I can't hit it hard enough. When I come to the net, people lob me to death. When I play from the baseline, they just overpower me."

John's father and his coach say his work ethic generally is good. He never gives up, even in losing situations against bigger opponents. He's been very conscientious about eating right, and for the last two years he's followed a modified weight-training program to help compensate for the size problem. "Nothing has helped much," John laments. "My father is 5 feet 3 inches and my mother is only 5 foot. Not only did I get a bad birthday, but I got bad genes, too."

John's feelings aren't unique. Hundreds of junior players find themselves pitted against opponents in their own age group who are considerably bigger and stronger. The cause may be developmental, genetic, hormonal, even nutritional. But the fact remains—they're small.

Is John's small-person complex inevitable when small meets big in the junior ranks? Is being a late bloomer always a curse?

Enter Paul "Killer" Kilderry.

Killer is special. Watch him play and words like "giant-killer" and "hit man" come to mind. Still, these hardly are adjectives one would associate with a 5-foot-4-inch, 15-year-old boy who weighs 118 pounds and looks like he couldn't be a day over 13.

"Who is that little kid?" asks a competitor as he sips his soda and watches Kilderry rip a backhand winner off a towering opponent's first serve during the Treasure Island tournament, a modest Florida west coast adult event. Kilderry goes on to lose in the semis.

"I love playing collegiate and men's tournaments," Kilderry says. "Players think it's a joke when I walk on the court. I often get some snide comment like, 'Can you see over the net?' I love it! I've actually found that the bigger and more macho my opponent, the better for me. I like being the small guy. People always think you're going to lose.

"Big guys get very intimidated when they play me," he adds. "I played all three legs of the Florida satellite tour last year, and I actually got comments like, 'This is a joke,' 'I can't lose to this little shrimp,' and 'If I lose to this muppet, I'll kill myself.'

"In one of the satellite matches my opponent glared at me for a moment when I hit a good shot, approached the net, pointed his finger at me, and said, 'I'll pound your head in if you hit one more lucky shot like that.'"

Size has never gotten in Kilderry's way. He was ranked No. 1 in the 14s in Australia in 1987. In 1986 he beat Tommy Ho, who later would win the Boys' 18 Nationals, in straight sets. And in the third round of the 1988 Orange Bowl he pinned a 6-0, 6-1 loss on Vincent Spadea, Jr., the No. 1-ranked 14-year-old in the U.S.

Until March of 1988, Paul couldn't play with a full-sized racket. He would have to chop one-and-a-half inches off the handle because it was too long and heavy. And if he seems small now, consider that for the past six months he's had a blazing growth spurt—nearly an inch a month.

What does Kilderry think about his new-found height? "Going from 4 feet 10 inches to 5 feet 4 inches so fast is great, I suppose," he says, "but I just hope I don't lose my mental edge over big guys."

Paul believes the advantages of being small far outweigh the disadvantages.

"I've been able to turn most of the obvious disadvantages into advantages," he says. "I don't have a big serve, so I never depend on my serve to win. Big guys always seem to play well if they serve well and play poorly if they serve poorly. I've really worked on my return because I know that if I can return a few of my opponents' big serves, they get very discouraged.

"Another disadvantage is my lack of strength. I can't overpower people. But that's been good because I've learned to work the points better. I used to get into trouble because I wanted to prove to my opponents I could hit the ball as hard as they could. We would start exchanging artillery and, although it looked impressive for a little guy to hit the ball that hard, I'd usually lose. Not being able to overpower people helped me learn better offensive and defensive strategies."

But don't be fooled by Kilderry's modesty. He effectively debunks the notion that small guys must push to win. Quite the contrary. He's an aggressive serve-and-volleyer with an array of offensive weapons.

"Small guys don't have to be pushers," Paul argues, "but they have to play smart. I've learned to generate pace by using my opponent's power rather than my own. Being small also has helped me to understand strategy and tactics better, and someday, when I do get some size, I think I'll be a smarter, all-around player.

"Because I'm so small, I have to run a lot more and cover a lot more court than my opponents. That's forced me to get into better shape and be fitter than big guys.

"Most big guys are slower than little guys, and I have speed and quickness on my side," he points out. "I'm also better balanced and can change direction more quickly because I'm closer to the ground and not carrying the weight."

Kilderry emphasizes that the real benefits to being small are mental, not physical.

"Because I was so small, I was never expected to win—just hang in there," he says. "If I lost to a bigger guy, I didn't feel so bad, but if my opponent lost to me, he always felt terrible. Being small takes the pressure off.

"I don't think small guys have to struggle with choking as much as big

Michael Chang is living proof that little guys can make it big.

guys. I never worried about winning that much because I was always working on things for the future, when I got some size. I think it's easier for little guys to go for their shots and not worry about winning."

Being small in the early years of tennis development may actually be a blessing. Make a list of all the advantages of being small. Start changing the way you think about your size. Don't look at it as a problem; use it to develop yourself into a complete player.

Are there any real drawbacks? Paul listed only three: he could never get good shoes that fit, his racket always hit the court on the follow-through when he served, and he couldn't reach high enough to shake the chair umpire's hand after he won the match.

CONFIDENCE GUIDE FOR LITTLE GUYS

1 Think of your size as an advantage, not a disadvantage. Being small forces you to work harder and develop all dimensions of your game.

2 Small doesn't necessarily mean weak. Develop a strength-training program.

3 Train hard aerobically. Be prepared to run down balls all day. Third sets are yours!

4 Work hard on your mental toughness. Little guys must be great fighters. No whining, complaining, or excuses.

5 Develop a powerful presence. Nothing is worse than a small guy who acts small.

6 Understand that size is not the determining factor in confidence. Viewed properly, being small can be a major confidence-builder.

10 REASONS WHY SMALL IS GREAT

1 It forces you to learn sound defensive, as well as offensive, strategies.

2 It inspires you to be fitter and in better shape because you run more.

3 It helps you learn to generate pace from your opponent's power.

4 It can give you a psychological edge against an overly confident opponent.

5 It prevents you from depending on your serve to win.

6 It encourages you to work to develop a good return of serve.

7 It generally means you are lighter, quicker, and faster.

8 Your lower center of gravity and slower growth often translate to better balance and coordination.

9 You aren't as likely to choke, because you feel less pressure to win.

10 It helps keep you focused more on development and less on winning or losing.

Monitoring Your Emotions

Learning to read and control your emotions is a valuable tool in mental-toughness training. If you are aware of the times when your fighting spirit is apt to desert you, and if you can harness your intensity and confidence, you'll have a distinct advantage over the player who allows his emotions to manipulate him.

Some players are incredible fighters. They're always coming at you; whether ahead or behind, playing well or poorly, they're like blood-hounds on a hot scent. Adverse conditions, bad luck, and unfair calls rarely dampen their spirit. They consistently overcome these obstacles with two emotional responses: they become challenged and remarkably persistent.

But there are other players who can't fight, who have no persistence whatsoever. Take Keith, a high school senior. He's talented, intelligent, comes from a good family with solid parents, and works very hard. He's motivated, competitive, and has received good coaching. He's got all the strokes and he looks terrific in practice.

But Keith is no fighter. When a match begins, a predictable pattern emerges. At the first sign of trouble, Keith starts to fade. His fighting spirit diminishes and is replaced by a curious sense of helplessness. He doesn't get crazed with anger; he just treads water and gets nowhere.

On closer examination, the real issue for Keith is that he doesn't believe in himself. He wants to win, but something in his background undermines his belief that he can perform, come back, or find an answer in the heat of battle. Why doesn't he believe? Why does Keith feel powerless during adverse competitive situations, while others rise to the occasion?

According to C. S. Dweck, Ph.D., a prominent researcher in sports psychology, helplessness stems from a faulty achievement pattern. Tennis players who respond to obstacles by feeling challenged and being persistent are *mastery-oriented*. They've learned to define their personal competency in terms of learning goals as opposed to outcome goals.

Learning goals are built around effort and outcome goals are built around final results, such as winning and losing.

The critical issue here is to control *learned helplessness,* which stems from consistent reinforcement of the notion that "I am not in control," that "whatever is going to happen will happen." The sense of powerlessness is commonly attributed to an athlete's lack of talent or ability. In Keith's case, as soon as adversity struck, feelings of incompetence and personal failure emerged as a result of Keith's self-perception of his poor natural ability.

Attributing one's failure in competition to a lack of ability typically leads to this learned pattern of helplessness. "If it's my ability that's the problem, there's little I can do," the player thinks.

The feeling of personal control is the key to the fighting spirit and persistence characteristic of top players. That feeling seems directly connected to the type of goals we set for ourselves as players.

When players are repeatedly exposed to what they perceive as uncontrollable outcomes, they eventually begin to feel two things. First, they believe that what ultimately happens in a match is beyond their control—it was the wind, bad luck, bad calls, poor lighting, or lousy court surface. Second, they feel they don't have the ability to successfully adjust their performance. This is the essence of learned helplessness. And the antidote for both the prevention and correction of this faulty emotional response is perceived success.

Success can be defined in any number of ways, but the kind of achievement goals we set for ourselves largely determine our ratio of success to failure. Players who set mastery or learning goals are likely to experience more perceived success, greater feelings of personal control, and less helplessness than those who set outcome goals. Mastery goals (often referred to as performance goals) deal with effort, learning, competence, and improvement; outcome goals deal with end results, final outcomes, and ultimate ends. Examples of mastery goals are learning to give 100 percent, learning to get more depth and spin on your second serve, learning to be more positive and aggressive during play, and learning to approach more on short balls. Examples of outcome goals are winning a specific game, match, or tournament, achieving specific local or national rankings, or beating a specific player.

Mastery goals enable you to carve out a sense of success even when you lose. Finding success in a losing effort helps prevent feelings of helplessness. You can't directly control winning, but you can always control your effort, attitude, sense of fight, and commitment to learning. By setting these kinds of performance goals, you begin to feel like every match you play can make a difference.

The following questions will help you determine whether learned helplessness is a problem for you.

1 When things don't go well for you during a match, do you think you are the problem (rather than your opponent)?

2 Will this same problem likely occur in future matches with this opponent?

3 Will this same problem likely occur in future matches with other opponents?

4 Do you feel your competitive problems are due to lack of ability?

5 Do you fight less or reduce your effort when things go badly during competition?

6 When things go badly, do you feel that nothing you can do will make a difference?

7 Are most of your goals during competition outcome-oriented (rather than performance- or mastery-oriented), and therefore not under your direct control?

8 Do you often have feelings of helplessness when things go badly in your matches?

The more yes answers you gave for these questions, the greater the likelihood that you're a victim of learned helplessness. And remember, skill level is not a factor here. The most highly skilled competitor is just as likely to struggle with this problem as the beginner.

Here are my suggestions:

1 Try to assess the extent to which learned helplessness is a competitive problem for you.

2 Understand that learned helplessness is directly tied to faulty achievement patterns that severely limit your ability to experience perceived success.

3 Begin to establish mastery goals for both practice and competition. Emphasis should be on improvement and learning rather than outcome.

4 Place the highest priority on effort, attitude, and strategy. Learning and improvement goals should supercede the importance of winning.

5 Every time you think you lack ability or the situation is beyond your control, say "*Stop!*" Renew your commitment to positive effort and attitude, and measure your success precisely in those terms.

6 Set daily mastery goals and keep an accurate record of the results. This will ensure a steady diet of success, the only real antidote to learned helplessness.

Upstaging the Letdown Phenomenon

While learned helplessness manifests itself as soon as the player faces a tough challenge, the "letdown phenomenon" can occur at almost any point in a match, even when the player is winning easily.

Ask most players why they lost a close match and you're likely to hear something about "letting down" as part of the explanation. Pros refer to it as often as club players. They make comments like, "I had the match on my strings, *let down,* and the whole thing turned around"; or "I finally got a break in the third and then *let down* on my serve and immediately got broken"; or "I upset the No. 2 seed in the first round and then *let down* and lost in the next round to some hack who couldn't even play."

An interesting example of this phenomenon was a match between Peter Fleming and David Wheaton, one of our nation's brightest juniors throughout the 1980s. Nationally ranked No. 2 in the 18s, Wheaton played a second-round qualifying match against Fleming to gain entry into the main draw of the Volvo Chicago tournament in March 1987. Wheaton won the first set 6-4 and felt he played well. According to David, he had a "letdown in the beginning of the second set" and quickly proceeded to lose that set 6-0. He got himself back together in the third and went up 3-0. Suddenly, the letdown phenomenon struck again. "I let down again, lost the next four games and the set 7-5," he admitted afterward.

A nearly identical scenario occurred one month later during a USTA Circuit Masters tournament in Georgia. Wheaton met satellite player Craig Campbell in the third round and won a hard-fought first set 7-5. Similar to the Fleming match, he was broken in the first game of the second set and lost 6-0. "I had a huge letdown again!" Wheaton lamented. In the third set he got an early break and, again, had another letdown. Campbell immediately broke back and went on to win the set and match 6-4.

Can all these sudden drops in performance really be related to the same thing? Is letting down the real culprit?

Letting down refers to a state of underactivation. It means the body is not sufficiently aroused to perform optimally. Using the analogy of an automobile engine, the RPMs are too low. In the body's case, the heart

Even top players like Stefan Edberg must fight feelings of helplessness.

rate, blood pressure, biochemical changes, etc., produce insufficient energy to perform well. It's often described by players and coaches in one word—intensity. Lost intensity is often equated with letting down. When players suddenly don't try as hard, and lack motivation or fight, letting down is the result.

The opposite of letting down is overarousal, overactivation. It is often the result of trying too hard. The player becomes too excited, too nervous, too angry; the RPMs pass the red line. The player begins forcing shots, racing too fast, going for too much.

It's been my experience that players often mistake problems of overarousal with those of letting down (underarousal). They look back at the match and, based on the score, assume they must have let down at critical points. An example would be Wheaton's loss to Fleming after achieving a 3-0 lead in the third set. Wheaton's poor play was not a case of underarousal, but overarousal due to nervousness. Synchronizing heart rate with a point-by-point computerized match analysis has helped us identify problems of letting down more clearly. Optimal arousal, though different for each person, generally corresponds to a particular range of heart rate. Players who experience sudden uncharacteristic drops in heart rate after they win a tough game or set are usually undergoing a letdown. Uncharacteristic increases in heart rate not attributable to exertion indicate overarousal.

Situation: You win a tough first set and immediately proceed to lose the next.

Is this a typical letdown? Answer: yes.

The heart rate of the winner of a hard-fought set often takes a dramatic drop immediately following the set. The player is greatly relieved to have won the set and his level of arousal reflects it.

Solution: After you win the first set, do everything you can to get fired up for the first game of the second set. If you have to pretend in your mind that you have lost the set, do so. Keep your feet moving, look energized, and keep the heart rate from dropping too low during the first and second games of the next set.

Situation: You are unseeded and beat the third seed in a tournament and then lose to a vastly inferior player in the next round.

Typical letdown? Answer: no.

Most players will experience higher stress and arousal levels when they play individuals of lesser perceived ability than their own. It's not threatening to lose to players better than you. Overarousal due to nervousness is the typical problem here.

Solution: Understand you'll feel much more pressure because now you're expected to win. Focus on being relaxed and calm, and take deep breaths and plenty of time between points. Pushing harder will generally make things worse.

Situation: You finally get the big break you've been working for and immediately proceed to lose your own serve.

Typical letdown? Answer: yes.

Over and again, we see players' heart rates take a major drop immediately after getting the big service break.

Solution: Make the game following the break the most important of the match. Note that heart rate may suddenly increase on occasion, particularly if the break occurred near the end of the match or set. When this occurs, pressure can suddenly increase and the solution would be to reduce arousal levels, as in the previous example.

Situation: You consistently lose games where you were ahead 30-0 or 40-0.

Typical letdown? Answer: no.

The closer you get to winning the game, the more pressure you feel.

Solution: Focus on relaxation, pace yourself, stay calm, and then be aggressive.

Situation: Ahead 5-2 in the third set, you start thinking about how great it's going to feel when you win . . . and then proceed to lose the match.

Typical letdown? Answer: yes.

Anticipation of victory generally reduces intensity and arousal.

Solution: Play one point at a time and resist thinking about the future, particularly when you're winning. Maintain the same intensity by focusing on the moment.

Situation: Ahead 5-2 in the third set, you start playing conservatively, your shots get shorter, and you end up losing the match.

Typical letdown? Answer: no.

Most people experience more pressure and arousal when they're ahead than behind. The closer you get to winning the game or match, the greater the tendency to start playing cautiously rather than aggressively. Conservative play combined with the increased arousal due to nervousness is the culprit.

Note: The difference between this situation and the previous one was *perceived* pressure. In the previous situation, the player experienced no increase in arousal toward the end of the set. In fact, thinking about how great it would be to win caused a decrease in arousal, which led to poor play.

Solution: Take plenty of time, don't rush, get very focused on what you want to do before each point. Regardless of how nervous you might feel, resist conservative play. Expect your opponent to play well near the end of the set because there's no pressure on him; but don't panic. A loss

David Wheaton has learned how to pump up at the right time to prevent a letdown.

of a game or two here is very common. If you resist getting discouraged and stay with your game plan, the pressure will resume building for your opponent and you'll likely win the set or match.

Situation: You and your partner lose in a local club doubles tournament to a team you should have beaten. You find yourself laughing and joking a lot during play. One of your opponents is a close personal friend you really like.

Typical letdown? Answer: yes.

In all likelihood, you have not taken this match seriously enough. You don't feel threatened or anxious because you're playing a friend. Your laughing and joking, although enjoyable, will only keep your arousal low. You may have difficulty getting competitive against a friend. If that happens, a letdown is likely.

Solution: Spend plenty of time preparing mentally for this match. Before the match, write down all the reasons you wouldn't want to lose to this team. Make yourself think about how it would feel if you lost. Make a commitment to give your best effort, and not talk or joke around during play. Save that for after the match. Set specific match goals.

Be very careful not to assume that letting down is the problem, and that trying harder is the answer. The question you should ask is, "How is my intensity changing?" Try to read your body's arousal changes. Are you too excited, or not enough so? Making the right determination is critical to solving the problem and getting your game back on track. As David Wheaton learned, unmasking the many faces of letting down can be the difference between winning and losing.

Positively Emotional

Of course you don't have to manipulate your emotions only to avoid negative situations like letdowns and learned helplessness. You can control your feelings to try to create an optimal emotional state that will help you play your best.

The words athletes choose when they describe their finest hours—let's call it their ideal performance state—often sound like Valley Girl–speak. Such descriptions as treed, zoned, maxed out, flow, psyched, jazzed, tranced, and pumped abound. In this state, athletes also talk about time standing still, extraordinary personal awareness, profound inner stillness, exceptional energy, and puzzling feelings of slow motion, joy, power, and control.

"I had tremendous intensity but was completely relaxed." "I was exceptionally calm inside but totally pumped with energy." "The situation was full of pressure, but I didn't feel any at all."

Despite the contradictory nature of these reports, obvious patterns emerge. After a time, it becomes evident that the mental state accompanying an outstanding performance is dramatically different from the mental state generally tied to a poor performance.

The single most important thing you can do to perform at your peak is to trigger this ideal performance state. Rest assured this special state is not the result of playing well; it is precisely what makes playing well possible. When you feel right, you can perform right, and controlling how you feel is a learned skill.

Zoning is really a question of emotional balance. It's an established fact that emotional changes produce measurable bodily and biochemical changes, some of which can lead to a variety of different altered states of consciousness. As your moods change during a match, so does your biochemistry. Only when your chemistry is right, when the mixture is rich and powerful, can you achieve maximum performance.

To achieve an ideal performance state, keep two important things in mind. First, when you're playing in "the zone," you are not in some far-out trance state. On the contrary, you're actually fine-tuned mentally.

Second, understand that your ideal performance state is controllable. Tennis' greatest competitors are the best examples, as they consistently turn in outstanding performances. Their greatness is due in part to their exceptional ability to control their ideal mental and emotional climate.

Players caught in the riptide of their own negative mood shifts during play can never achieve their potential. For them, "zoning" is only something that sporadically happens by chance.

If you want to start controlling your ideal mental climate, here are three suggestions:

Increase Awareness.   Start tuning in to what mental and emotional climate is associated with your best performances. How do you feel when you're really playing well? What is the best combination of winning feelings for you? Once your ideal climate is familiar, you are ready to begin mental and emotional fine-tuning.

Use Your Positive Emotions as Fuel.   Fueling your performances with positive emotions is the best way to get the right chemistry going. When challenge, enthusiasm, and determination are replaced by anger, frustration, or fear, emotional fine-tuning is impossible.

Model Yourself After Outstanding Competitors.   Once again, Jimmy Connors and Martina Navratilova are great players to emulate.

Great competitors always outwardly project the same feelings that we now know are connected to high-level performance. They project relaxation, calmness, low pressure, high positive intensity, and confidence.

Two words of caution. First, controlling your ideal performance state is a never-ending process. You improve by inches and fractions of inches, not yards. It is truly the greatest challenge in sport. Second, zoning mentally does not guarantee that you will zone physically. There are a host of physical factors that can block the path, like fatigue, sickness, and diet. Zoning mentally simply allows you to play to the limits of your physical skill and talent.

Chapter II

YOUR NERVOUS
SYSTEM:
RESPONDING TO
PRESSURE

Competition is nothing more than a series of problems: wind, opponents who cheat, heat, late starts, lousy courts, equipment breakdowns, poor lighting. Every time you double-fault, lose your serve, miss a sitter, pull a muscle, or when momentum shifts in a match, it's a problem. The key to mental toughness is how you respond emotionally to problems.

Competition puts our self-esteem on the line; we often take a psychological risk when we compete. We risk looking bad; losing to someone we shouldn't; disappointing coaches, parents, and friends; losing peer prestige or rankings; and the list goes on. Problems encountered during match play can trigger powerful emotions because the perceived psychological stakes are often very high.

There are four general types of responses that typify the way we emotionally respond to problems during match play:

The Tanking Response. One of the first ways players learn to respond emotionally to problems is to tank. By withdrawing effort and commitment, they psychologically distance themselves from the activity and experience less pain and agony and less of a threat to their self-esteem. Players often explain bad losses by saying, "I just wasn't in it today" or, "If I had *really* tried, I would have won." If you give less than 100 percent and lose, you still have a psychological way out. You lost not because your opponent was better but because you didn't try hard enough. As long as players allow themselves the option of tanking when things get tough, their development is halted.

The Temper Response.   After players close the psychological escape hatch of tanking, the next obstacle they usually must face is temper or anger. Players frequently explain bad losses by saying that they simply "lost it emotionally"—they went crazy with anger or rage and, as a result, their level of play wasn't indicative of what they could really do. This way, players can again shield themselves from the uncomfortable and unacceptable reality of what actually happened. Temper and anger are also often used to communicate to opponents and those watching that you aren't really that bad, that this is just a really bad day for you. "If I continue to play without showing any negative emotion, people will think this is how terrible I really am!"

The temper response is one step above tanking because you're still ego-involved but you'll never reach your competitive potential until that option is effectively shut down.

The Choking Response.   When players close the psychological escape routes of tanking and temper, the next obstacle they face is choking. In an important sense, choking is an indication of something very positive. It is two steps ahead of tanking and one step ahead of temper in the development of mental toughness. When players choke, it means they are very involved in what they're doing. They're taking risks, putting their egos on the line. For players with a history of tanking and temper problems, choking is a sign of real progress. Players will eventually learn to manage the choking response effectively, as long as they don't regress to tanking or temper responses again. The more opportunities players have in learning to manage pressure and crises constructively, the quicker they will break through. So long as tanking and temper are allowable options, mastery of choking is definitely prolonged.

The Challenge Response.   The final stage of mental toughness is reflected in the challenge response. You actually find yourself investing more positive intensity, more of yourself as the situation gets tougher. You find that the problems you face in competition are not threatening but stimulating. You've gone well beyond simply loving to win. You have clearly come to *love the battle*. As a result of this emotional response, you become an excellent problem solver. When everyone else is heading for the trenches as the problems start mounting, you smile inside because you know you've got the emotional edge.

Martina Navratilova projects the image of a great champion: confidence and intensity combined with relaxation and calmness.

Temper Your Tantrums On-Court

Players who respond to pressure with temper tantrums have a special problem when trying to modify their behavior. Even though they hate the embarrassment of creating a scene, they can't control themselves, which makes the whole situation even *more* frustrating. Amy Schwartz, who in 1984 won the Easter Bowl 16s, the Florida State Closed and was runner-up at the National 16 Clay Courts, had a familiar story to tell. She, like so many developing players, had struggled for years to control her temper. "I hate myself when I lose it," she said. "I start acting like a jerk and then feel stupid."

As with most players with temper problems, Amy's parents, coaches, and friends pleaded with her to learn to tame the lion inside. "I knew they were right," Schwartz said, "but I couldn't stop it.

"The same thing always happens. As pressure starts building, I start getting more impatient and negative with myself until eventually my thoughts and anger take control. It's all over after that."

However, when Amy tried not to get angry, she would become emotionally dead inside: "I just couldn't get fired up and I'd start choking and playing real tentative. Eventually I would start getting mad again and start playing better. But it never lasted. I never play great when I get angry."

An important dynamic of players with temper problems is often that they are fiercely competitive. They literally have a rage to win. "I can't stand to lose," Amy said. "Maybe I want to win too badly. As soon as it looks like I might lose, I start to boil inside."

Temper problems can create considerable self-condemnation, guilt, embarrassment, and confusion for a player. Haunting feelings of "Why can't I stop?", "What's the matter with me?", and "Why can't I control myself?" often cut deeply into a player's psyche. Athletes are often left with the feeling that, no matter how hard they try, the whole thing is beyond them.

Over the past 10 years, sports psychologists have made some important discoveries about nervousness that we can all apply to our games. The first is that the feeling of nervousness is uncomfortable and unpleasant for most players. Nerves means fear, and fear means scary. And when scary is for real, it's no fun. Fear makes us want to run away, to remove ourselves, to hide. Feeling helpless and lost are common side effects of the emotion of fear. Most players would quickly choose anger over fear. Anger is generally perceived as less unpleasant than nervousness, and players feel less victimized and helpless.

The second discovery is that players resort to all kinds of mental and emotional strategies—many of which are very counterproductive—to avoid being nervous. The two most common are getting angry and upset (temper tantrums), and giving up by withdrawing emotional involvement and effort (tanking). It's important for players to understand how their temper is often linked to nervousness.

Players who frequently tank or show temper often report that they rarely feel nervous during match play. They've successfully eliminated nervousness, but the price is highly inconsistent, poor play. Most players have never made the conscious connections in their mind between their temper, tanking, and nervousness. It's an important connection.

The third discovery is that most players change their style of play when they get nervous. Most do one of two things: they either push the ball and play very tentatively or start overhitting and go for first- or second-ball winners. Pushing the ball is the most common. Nervousness leads to tighter muscles, causing one's strokes to get shorter, more restricted, and jerky. Players just try to keep the ball in play in the hope that their opponent will miss, because they feel they no longer can hit the ball the way they like. They start playing not to lose rather than to win. Their strategy for handling nervousness is simply not to miss. This highly defensive style translates into shorter balls, less variety, and no power. Pushing will lead to an occasional victory, but pushers rarely make all-around good competitors. And even when you win, you often feel badly about the match because even though pushing worked this time, you know there's no future in it.

Those who overhit when nervous are often the ones who win big or lose big. Their answer to the nervousness is to go for it! "I hate to push, so when I get tight I nail it. If it goes in, great. If not, at least I didn't push it." Unfortunately, neither pushing nor pounding the ball as a strategy for nervousness will result in long-standing success. The best players in the game today clearly respond to nervousness in a different way.

So what can players do to control their nerves—and their temper?

Start by filming your matches. It was a real shock to Schwartz when she saw for the first time on video tape what she looked like as she got negative and angry during tournament play. The shock of seeing what you look like during bad times can have a very positive effect.

Next, reduce the pressure to win without putting out the fire. For Amy, the goal of winning at any cost was replaced with playing the very best she could at every moment. Simply focus on giving 100 percent physically and emotionally on every point, and let winning take care of itself.

Tie match success to your ability to project a powerful, positive, and

Master of the Challenge Response, Chris Evert is the picture of control.

calm physical image during crisis situations. If mistakes, line calls, or bad luck start to trigger anger, continue to project a strong image of positive determination and calmness.

Mentally rehearse how you want to handle crisis and adversity, both from an emotional and a physical perspective, daily. See yourself perform and feel the way you want to feel. Try to think of yourself as a confident fighter tempered with unshatterable emotional control.

Lastly, adopt a strategy that will produce the results you want. The answer is *not* to simply never get nervous, because you can't unless you tank or go crazy with anger. The idea is to have a definite plan and follow it. From my experience and research with players, the following five-step formula produces the best long-term results:

Step 1:   Acknowledge that you're starting to get nervous.

Step 2:   Take more time doing everything between points. Slow down and make sure you don't rush.

Step 3:   Get more ritualistic. Stay with your rituals—bouncing the ball, swaying back and forth, blowing on your hand, and visualizing what you want to do on the next point.

Step 4:   Take at least one deep breath before the start of the point.

Step 5:   Play high-percentage, aggressive tennis.

Step 5 is the toughest. It takes courage and commitment. High-percentage aggressive tennis means playing aggressively but consistently. It means not pushing and not going for first- or second-ball winners. It means hitting the ball with depth and pace, but not going for lines and low-percentage shots. It's hitting your first serve at 70- to 80-percent pace rather than going for the ace. It's hitting the approach shot aggressively and coming in rather than going for the outright winner. It's attacking with the fewest unforced errors. Your goal is to put pressure on your opponent, to get him or her to make a forced error. When nervous and unsure of yourself, make your opponent hit the tough pass rather than the reverse. Make things happen rather than wait for them to happen. This style generally means more topspin, more cross-courts, no drop shots, coming to the net on short balls, and hitting the ball aggressively. Your goal is to play a style that will lead to forced errors by your opponent but, at the same time, keep your unforced errors to a minimum. And if you should lose the point or the match, continue to stay with your goal of high-percentage, aggressive tennis because in the long haul, it will make you a tougher competitor.

To make the formula work, keep these things in mind:

- Develop a second serve that rarely fails under pressure. To be a good pressure player, you should have a second serve that can be hit aggressively and with consistency.

- Strokes that always collapse when you get nervous need to be re-tooled. Your strokes must allow you to still play aggressively when you're nervous and tight.

- Don't allow yourself to use tanking and temper to cool your nervousness. They are both false answers.

- Never be afraid to be nervous—despite how uncomfortable and disruptive it can sometimes be. It's a sign you're in the match emotionally and that you care. When it happens, play aggressive and smart tennis and continue to love the battle.

The road to properly taming one's temper is never a straight line. It's always spotted by temporary breakdowns and detours. If Amy failed to meet her goal for a match, set, or point, her assignment was simply to clear her mind as quickly as possible and renew her commitment to success.

Schwartz will quickly tell you that it wasn't easy. But after her string of successes in 1984, she came to know that the choice was really hers. "I now know that I can do it," Amy said. "But I also know that I must work on it every day or it all fades away. I've already learned that if I don't constantly work on it, my old habits are right there to defeat me again."

Putting Your Ego on the Line

If you've had problems with tanking or temper tantrums, choking is a sign that you've turned the corner and are headed for the homestretch. The challenge response, that positive, productive response to pressure, awaits at the finish line. But first you have to get over this last hurdle.

Your muscles are braced, stomach is churning, and adrenaline pumping. You are mobilized for a life-or-death struggle. But the confrontation is hardly life or death, it's simply a third-set tiebreaker you don't want to lose. Choking is out of the question. What's needed now is calmness and looseness.

Choking is nothing more than letting your body do the right thing at the wrong time. Your biological alarm, which serves to perpetuate life, has gone off. You perceive the situation as life-threatening, but, in reality, the only stakes in the match are pride, prestige, and sometimes money.

As to the question of who chokes, the answer is *everyone*—from the best to the worst. At the highest levels of the game, choking can be seen as John McEnroe grabs his throat and drops to his knees after dumping an easy break point into the net; as Martina Navratilova loses to Zina Garrison at the 1987 U.S. Open; and as Jimmy Arias loses the deciding Davis Cup match against Paraguay in 1987 after leading 5-2 in the fifth set.

It's actually a very costly mistake to believe good competitors never choke. If that's the rule of thumb you're using to define your own success as a competitor, you're likely to always be dissatisfied. Great competitors do choke, but they do it rarely and, when it happens, it's not likely to seriously undermine their confidence or concentration.

Choking takes a variety of intriguing and perplexing forms. A full-scale alarm can produce considerable confusion, steeled muscles, poor balance, negative thinking, and body shakes. In another context, rubbery knees; short, tentative strokes; and shallow, irregular breathing may be the pattern. Subtle choking often takes the form of trying too hard on big points or rushing and forcing the point.

It's interesting to note how players react to mistakes versus choking. To miss a forehand is one thing, but to choke a forehand, well, that's another matter entirely. For whatever reason, choking a shot seems to be much more personal, and if you ever get labeled a choker, things can get very rough. A good example is Dennis Van der Meer, who at one time was a promising South African junior. In a critical Davis Cup match, Van der Meer squandered several match points and, after losing, became labeled as a choker by his peers. Unfortunately there was no effective remedy for Van der Meer's problem at that time. Unaware of how to deal with such a dilemma, Dennis began to repeatedly fold in tight situations until he had to end his career as a player at age 20.

Today things are different. There are many strategies for controlling choking that have proved very useful to players. Here are my top 10:

Don't set out *not* to choke.   The more obsessed you are about not choking, the worse things usually get. Develop the attitude that, if you choke, you choke, and then you simply move on. Always set goals to do something positive in your match, like staying enthusiastic, giving 100 percent on every point, and being aggressive. Never strive not to achieve something.

Play every point as though it were the most important one of the match.   If every point is of the same importance, there should be no such thing as big points. Every point should get your maximum effort, and every point is a pressure point. Soon you will start handling the pressure better. There's no better model than Jimmy Connors for this strategy.

The tougher the situation, the more you should love it.   Pressure is what triggers choking. Getting inspired when your back is against the wall is what transforms that pressure into productive energy. Few people could do this better than Billie Jean King. If you're loving it, choking is out of the question.

When in doubt, go for it!   Rod Laver was a master. When things got tight, you could count on him to go for it. When things get shaky, it's better to be aggressive than safe. If you hit with topspin, all the better.

Improve your strokes that fold under pressure.   If your serve is the first thing to go, modify your technique and increase your margin for error. If the same stroke always goes south, it's more likely that the stroke needs fixing, not your head.

Focus on each point, one at a time.   Bjorn Borg, the iron man of tennis, considered this the absolute key to his success. He worked hard to play each point as though it were his first and last. There was no past or future; there was only the present.

Set a simple game plan with clear options and stick to it. When Arthur Ashe stepped onto a court, he nearly always had a game plan and felt mentally prepared. There is no substitute for doing your homework before you play. It's amazing how that helps to take the pressure off.

Get a good workout in just before your match.   A good sweat will help break down muscle tension. Consider a short run to get that calm and loose feeling. If you're still feeling tight, nail the first few balls to break the tension.

Take plenty of time doing everything, particularly your rituals.   Invariably, players start speeding up as the pressure mounts. Make every effort to resist the urge to rush. Imagine yourself in slow motion between points.

Above all, make up your mind to have fun!   This simple attitude can make all the difference. Try it.

Exhaling Anxiety Away

Take a deep breath. This is perhaps one of the simplest, most instinctive ways man knows of to fight nervousness. Once he's frightened, his heart racing and his brain considering the option of fleeing, man pauses and takes a very deep breath. Then, a little calmer, he can face his foe head-on.

Breathing is a window to our emotions. Happy or sad, nervous or challenged, breathing patterns fluctuate as our feelings change. We can, though, alter our feeling states and corresponding physical states by controlling the way in which we breathe, especially on court. Here are three tips that can help your performance level:

1 Get your breathing perfectly synchronized with your hitting during points. Breathe in as the ball comes to you and breathe out precisely at the point of contact. Breathe through the mouth at contact point; let the flow of air be aggressive and long. If you are doing it properly, you will make a long *ahhhh* sound as you hit. The longer and more powerful the breath, the better you'll control your breathing. It is most important that your breathing is in precise rhythm with your hitting. You will actually get the feeling that you are attacking the ball with your breath. To learn this breathing pattern, pronounce the word *yessss* at the exact point of contact in practice. An auditory cue will make the learning process much simpler. If you are a breath holder, and many are, it will generally take two to three weeks of practice to get your breathing synchronized.

   Your muscles will be more relaxed (your muscles are more relaxed as you exhale), ensuring that you're taking in sufficient oxygen during points. You'll also maintain a definite rhythm during play, helping you to be more aggressive because you are attacking the ball with your breathing. Lastly, this method of breathing will help keep your strokes long and full (when your breath is long and smooth during the follow-through, it's more difficult to have short, jerky strokes).

2 Take at least one deep breath from your lower stomach before starting a point whenever you're feeling angry, frustrated, or feeling the pressure of play. Breathe in through your nose and out through your mouth. As you bring air in, raise your shoulders up and then drop them completely as you exhale through your mouth with a long, continuous flow of air.

3 During changeovers, inhale slowly through your nose to a count of four, hold for two seconds and then slowly exhale through your

Even pros such as Henri Leconte get nervous and tight. No one is immune.

mouth to a count of four. This will get you relaxed, keep you focused, and help you better deal with the pressures of play. And perhaps help you win more points on court.

Avoiding the Extremist Trap

On-court behavior in tennis can be peculiar, colorful, entertaining, and unpredictable, but more than any other attribute, it's always uniquely personal. Why? Because we all get nervous at times, and each of us will do whatever it takes, no matter how uncharacteristic of our usual off-court behavior, to stop those nerves from making us feel uncomfortable and hurting our play.

Extremist positions in tennis often reveal personal insecurities, vulnerabilities, and weaknesses. Such positions typically result from the merging of personality dynamics with the pressure demands of the sport. Developing extremist styles on court in such areas as intimidation, emotionality, socialization, introversion, and self-analysis may help meet personal needs and insecurities, but may cost you dearly in terms of your tennis development.

We must find new ways of meeting those important psychological needs and of managing on-court pressure so that our tennis can continue to prosper and grow. And the answer for most people is not a dramatic, total personality reversal. Gradual, progressive changes reflecting a more balanced, less extreme position will often lead to competitive breakthroughs. It's really a matter of degree. Let's examine some extremist traps common to tennis players. Each represents a continuum.

The Shell. *What you do:* You show absolutely no emotion on court. Neither spectators nor opponents have any real clue as to your real personality. You seem unaffected by everything. You are emotionless whether you win or lose the point. Tennis doesn't appear to be much fun, only something you endure. As the pressure mounts, your tendency is to retreat even more into your shell.

How you think: "I don't like to show my personality on-court. I'm uncomfortable and embarrassed when I show emotion. Sometimes I envy players who are totally themselves on-court, but that's not me."

Favorite opponents: Players who also show no emotion on-court. Players who display emotions freely are often very intimidating to Shells.

Weakness: Emotion brings energy, fight, arousal, and determination. Shutting out emotion, particularly positive emotion, typically translates into uninspired, low-intensity play. Allowing your personality to emerge on-court, particularly in positive ways, brings life, fun, and spontaneity to your play.

Breathing out at contact helps Aaron Krickstein prevent choking.

The Psycho.   *What you do:* Every feeling and emotion you experience shows. Your personality is completely transparent on court and, since emotions can change so dramatically during play, you vault from rage to joy or from boredom to fear. You're on an emotional roller coaster and everybody can see it.

How you think: "It's important that I be myself out there. I'm just an emotional person and for me to be anything else would be very unnatural and phony. I've tried to keep my emotions in more, but it never works."

Favorite opponents: Psychos love to play Shells because they can intimidate them right out of the match with their wild personality swings. The Shells get terribly angry with Psychos, but never show it.

Weakness: Being on an emotional roller coaster typically means being on a performance roller coaster as well. The outward expressions of emotions, particularly negative emotions, often exaggerate the physiological effects of the emotion and reinforce its recurrence. Performance consistency is nearly impossible in combination with dramatic shifts in emotion.

The Court Jester.   *What you do:* Always talking, laughing, sympathizing, and socializing during play, you're overly nice, sweet, friendly, and accommodating. You rarely show competitiveness and would much rather lose a match than a friend. You're always complaining about your inability to concentrate.

How you think: "I don't think it's possible to be a good friend and also highly competitive. Sure, I like to win, but I'm not going to risk any friendships over it. I enjoy the people and social aspects more than the competition. I don't think it's too healthy to be so competitive."

Favorite opponents: Court Jesters love to play other Court Jesters. For them, this represents the ultimate in competition.

Weakness: Court Jesters find it nearly impossible to generate any intensity, spirit, or aggression. As a consequence, they rarely compete well and have great trouble concentrating. These individuals silently suffer great frustration, since they want to win, but can't.

The Intimidator.   *What you do:* You treat your opponent as the enemy. You stare, point your finger, threaten, and look for any opportunity to engage in psychological battle. Close calls that go against you are perfect opportunities for psychological warfare. Even when you play your friends, your personality is suddenly transformed into a Darth Vader reproduction.

How you think: "I have to hate my opponent to play well. I can't be a nice guy and win. I play like a dog when I'm nice. I'd rather win than make friends. All my friends know that I'm an animal on-court, but a nice guy off-court. If I can just find a reason to hate my opponent, I play better."

Favorite opponents: The Intimidator doesn't really care, but is totally turned off by the Court Jester. This type of person drives him crazy on-court.

Weakness: Anger does raise intensity levels but is also very hard to control. Too much anger causes muscle tightness, poor concentration, and excess aggression. Many players fall into this trap, but gradually learn that it's not the hatred that's the key, but rather the arousal. And arousal from positive emotions is just as powerful, but promotes greater consistency, better control, and more enjoyment. The old belief that you have to hate your opponent to play well is clearly a myth.

The No-Brainer. *What you do:* You shoot from the hip and play totally by instinct. Your play is best described as spontaneous, automatic, and, at times, very unintelligent. Your opponents find you very unpredictable—with good reason. Even you aren't sure what you'll do next. Whatever happens, happens.

How you think: "I don't like to think on-court. It just confuses me. The more I think the worse I get. I like to leave my brain in the locker room. I play better that way."

Favorite opponents: It doesn't really make any difference who the No-Brainer is up against because his style of play has no logical connection to that of his opponents. How he plays each match is as much a surprise to him as everyone else.

Weakness: The No-Brainer often plays very unintelligent tennis. He's typically a very poor problem solver on-court and often employs the worst possible strategy against his opponents. When things go wrong, when a stroke breaks down, for example, he often has no idea how to correct the situation.

The Analyst. *What you do:* There's a reason for everything and you're going to find it. Your play is controlled, calculated, and measured. You rarely do anything stupid, but your play appears very mechanical and uncreative. You project the look of a robot. Every mistake produces a complete analysis of stroke failure followed by a detailed prescription of what to do next.

How you think: "Intelligence and logic always prevail. Tennis is much like chess—better thinking means better play." Many Analysts also feel that their games will self-destruct if they don't hold them together with rational thought.

Favorite opponents: Analysts love to play No-Brainers. Their intelligent style will more often than not defeat pure athleticism.

Weakness: The price of being overly analytical is the loss of your natural athleticism. The body's natural flow, rhythm, and grace are short-circuited by overthinking. Although this style of play is intelligent, execution is rigid, unnatural, and highly predictable. Analysts frequently have problems with muscle tightness as pressure mounts.

The Crusher.   *What you do:* Under pressure you get wildly aggressive and start hitting harder and harder. You punish the ball. You go for the big winner—fast! You either win big or lose big. (And you lose more than you win.) Your answer to any problem is "Attack!"

How you think: "I'm a hitter. I'd rather hit hard and lose than push the ball and win. Hitting *hard* is what makes the game fun for me. I hate pushers. They're cowards. I have no respect for them. They should be forced to play in their own separate tournaments."

Favorite opponents: Opponents who play just like you do. You love to play big hitters. You always play well against them and always have fun.

Weakness: You often lose to pushers. You have real trouble with players who are highly consistent and give you no pace. Your opponents know that all they have to do is keep balls in play and you will error yourself out of the match. Everyone tries to push when they play you.

The Twinkie.   *What you do:* Under pressure you get everything back. You become the ultimate retriever. Your balls are hit with no pace, clear the net by 10 feet, and generally land around the center of the court. You are a masterful lobber, are generally in great shape, and love to run.

How you think: "If I have to hit a thousand balls to win the point, I will. I don't care if I don't hit the ball hard. I'm into winning. I love to tear apart big hitters' games. I don't care how I look or who I impress—I'd rather win than look good."

Favorite opponents: You like to take on opponents who hit big and have little patience (Crushers). You love knocking these big guns down to size. Who you don't like to play is someone just like you. Even when you win 6-0, 6-2, the match is likely to last three hours.

Weakness: You have trouble with smart, attacking players. Players with good overheads force you to pass and you've been hitting no-pace shots for so long, it's difficult to hit effective passing shots. Your game will win you a lot of trophies—up to a certain level. Then you will find success only by incorporating more aggressive tactics into your game.

How can you change? The first step is to acknowledge your extremist position and to understand that you have acquired it because it has been helpful, to a certain extent. The next step is to determine how this position hurts you. How much competitive success does it cost you? Specifically list the negatives on paper. The third step is to make a commitment to move toward a more balanced position. Give yourself six months to see major progress. Growth is generally gradual and subtle. The real key is to define specific behaviors to execute during matches that reflect this change. Some examples: The Shell may agree to call lines more loudly, say "yes" out loud occasionally after a good shot, and stand taller with head up; conversely, the Court Jester may decide not to say anything except the score between points or games.

Be Your Own Best Fan

Another common extremist style is the Self-Berater—the player who tells himself, "You stink!" after every lost point. Sometimes he speaks to himself negatively even when he's playing well and winning.

Why does the Self-Berater's game seem to depend upon his negative and critical attitude? A fundamental psychological principle is that all behavior is purposeful. Players act, think, and talk negatively because it serves a purpose. It is in one or more ways reinforcing for the player to be negative. If the negativism wasn't helpful in some ways, the player wouldn't do it. Sometimes the Self-Berater plays better when he's negative rather than positive because this is the way he's learned to deal with competitive pressure. The critical issue is that the player seems to get more nervous when he's positive.

As players start entering competition, they consciously and unconsciously begin exploring strategies to control their nerves. Most players quickly discover that being pessimistic reduces pressure. Players who get excessively negative on court rarely get nervous. They have learned a strategy to control their nervousness, so when they try to be positive, they often feel uncomfortable and play poorly. Being positive and telling yourself, "I can do it," often increases feelings of pressure. On the other hand, negative feelings—telling yourself you'll never do it or you're worthless—take the pressure off. You don't expect anything from yourself because you're so bad, so when you prepare to serve or receive you're less likely to be nervous.

Over time, those negative patterns can become extremely resistant to change, particularly in highly competitive individuals. In spite of all the urgings and even threats by coaches and parents, the negative patterns persist because they work. But the problem is, they only work so far.

Being negative will temporarily reduce the pressure, but this strategy undermines so many other critical performance factors that long-term success is rarely possible. From a spectator's perspective, the solution is so easy: just be more positive and you'll be great. That in fact is true, but the issue is far more difficult and complex for most people.

Here are my suggestions for Self-Beraters:

- Understand that you are negative because it helps reduce pressure. As long as you allow yourself to reduce pressure with this strategy, your growth as a competitor will be blocked and your skill as a player will never fully develop. Equally important, your joy in playing the game will be diminished.

- Changing your negative responses to positive ones will take time and effort. Changing your negativism must assume much greater importance than winning during the relearning phase. Plan on being nervous as you try to be more positive. At times you'll not play as well and you'll be uncomfortable, but this will force you to deal with pressure in a more constructive, positive way. For example, you'll learn how to use the challenge response and how to fight by using your positive emotions.

- List all your on-court negative responses. Be as specific as possible. For example: I roll my eyes and shake my head when I make a mistake. For every negative response, describe a positive replacement. Example: I will keep my eyes straight ahead and my head still. Be sure to list all your negative self-talk. Then make a list of the things that you are allowed to say that should be helpful. Examples might be "Let it go" after a mistake, "Calm down, slow down" if you're too nervous, or "Come on!" if you're too sluggish.

- Grade yourself after each match or practice. Be tough on yourself if you don't perform positively as you define it. Winning will come when the new positive responses become habits. Only then will you realize your full potential as a player.

It's Not *All* in Your Head

You can pin a lot of things on nerves, but you can also go too far. People often complain that the jitters make them double-fault on important points.

I understand. Nothing is more agonizing to competitors than double-faulting. Most feel that the reason they constantly double-fault under pressure is that they're chokers. It's very important that players understand the problem is not a mental but a mechanical one. If a stroke consistently breaks down under pressure, it's not your head that needs fixing, it's the stroke.

If you double-fault often on key points, you probably practice your second serve very rarely and never get specific help for this part of your game. My recommendation is to get a good teaching pro and start working on the second serve. Try a good spin serve, which has a substantial margin of error, yet can be hit aggressively. Once you can do that, your "mental problem" should vanish.

Chapter III

THE STRESS FACTOR: GUARDING AGAINST ANXIETY

In 15 years as a sports psychologist, I have worked in a wide variety of sports. They include hockey, basketball, football, soccer, gymnastics, figure skating, golf, swimming, running—both long and short distance—most racket sports, and even pistol shooting, archery, and boxing. Every sport has its own set of unique physical and mental demands. Without question, in my experience, tennis is the toughest of all from an emotional perspective.

When you examine all the relevant factors in tennis, the reasons why this game creates such a pressure-cooker effect become evident:

- Tennis is an individual sport. Individual sports generally produce more pressure than team sports for participants.

- There are no substitutes and no timeouts. No one can take your place momentarily until you get yourself together.

- There is no coaching. Except in collegiate tennis and the Davis and Federation cups, no one can help you. You are truly alone. You either make it or break it on your own merit.

- Your opponent makes the judgment as to whether your ball is in or out. In most instances, players must serve as their own referees. You can hit the ball squarely in the court for a winner on the most important point in the match and have the opponent call the ball out and you have virtually no recourse. This places tremendous emotional pressure on players.

- You face a real, physical opponent. Unlike many individual sports, such as gymnastics and figure skating, you are directly in combat with another person. The face-to-face interaction with an opponent adds enormously to the pressure dynamics.

- The scoring system means you're never safe. You cannot build a big lead and wait for the clock to run out. There is no clock; you are always vulnerable.

- The length of matches and varying conditions can be exhausting. The pressure dynamics of having to concentrate for such extended periods of time are extraordinary. Subtle changes in wind, lighting, court surface, noise, and altitude can have a pronounced effect on the physics of the game, and create significant emotional obstacles.

- There's nowhere to hide. Tennis creates a dramatically visible arena where everything you do and say is public business. When things start to fall apart, everyone knows.

- Parents are overly involved from the start. Because of the complex nature of the game and the significant dollars and time required for success, parents get overinvolved very quickly. Few factors produce more lethal pressure on players, young players, than that generated by parents.

- Self-esteem is squarely on the line. To achieve elite status in tennis, players must start early and devote a significant portion of their life to the game. It becomes extremely difficult for players to separate who they are from how they are doing. To maintain a perspective that "this is just a game" becomes increasingly less likely.

Even under the best circumstances, tennis can be rough. Everyone at some point finds the game taking them beyond their limits. The pressure cooker can bring the strongest to their knees.

Such was the case with one of our nation's most promising young juniors. Marco Cacopardo has always been an excellent competitor. In 1986 he was a top nationally ranked 16-and-under player who had managed the pressure of competition well, according to his parents. But, as inevitably happens, Marco was treated to an extra-special dose of what we call pressure.

It all began at the Junior Davis Cup tryouts in July 1986. Marco was

John McEnroe is back with a new attitude and a new, more positive approach to the game. According to John, it makes the game more fun.

playing well, winning matches, cruising. And then, out of the blue, it happened. Playing a pivotal match against Martin Blackman to make the team, Marco led 5-2 in the third set, serving at 40-15. Suddenly, he became so nervous he could hardly move. His muscles tightened, his heart raced out of control, the chemistry of fear dominated his physiology.

Marco lost the third set and match 7-5. He never won another game once the pressure hit him.

From the Junior Davis Cup tryouts, Marco went to the Boys' 16 National Hard Courts. He was seeded sixth. The pressure hit again. Marco lost in the first round to an unseeded player in straight sets.

"I couldn't hold on to my racket," he said. "I couldn't move my feet. I felt paralyzed and lost. I couldn't even call balls out. I would open my mouth and nothing would come out. I was so scared I couldn't believe it."

After the match Marco felt lower than ever. "I felt like totally quitting the game. I honestly believed I couldn't play the game any more. My future was over."

Marco's parents also witnessed his agony. "We had never seen anything like that before," said his mother, Sheila. "We felt helpless and very concerned."

After consulting with his parents, Marco withdrew from the tournament, shaken and confused. The game had struck again.

Marco returned home to Forest Hills, New York, and started a process of rebuilding. He talked, thought, and worked.

When a player loses confidence so dramatically and suddenly, the confusion, self-doubt, and even guilt can be devastating. As Marco found: "I no longer felt the same about myself or the game. It was like I lost my ability to play, and I no longer saw playing as fun."

What was fun, challenging, and exciting suddenly became threatening and scary. And this is precisely when coaches, parents, and special friends need to be there. Without some outside help and perspective, players can drift for months from such episodes. I have personally encountered players who have been literally stuck for years, stemming from a poorly managed, perceived failure.

What did Marco do to get emotionally back on track? Perhaps most important, Marco talked about his feelings openly with his parents, special friends, and coaches. The coaches at the Nick Bollettieri Tennis Academy, where he trains in Florida, could clearly see his personal struggle. Fortunately, Marco didn't bottle everything up inside and try to hide or deny what was happening, as many players do. Players often don't want to reveal any weakness or flaws in their armor, so they fight the battle totally alone.

This is generally one of the worst personal strategies players can use.

What is needed is a new perspective on the event. In Marco's case, he needed to reevaluate the importance of the Junior Davis Cup tryouts and the Nationals. He needed support, encouragement, and a new definition of those events. The best chance of that happening was when he opened up and discussed them with special people.

Parents play a critical role in properly managing this type of situation; Marco's parents did exactly the right thing. They took the pressure off completely: they listened, understood, accepted, and never judged. Although they didn't understand what was happening, they just went with the feelings Marco had.

"Marco's feelings were first and foremost, and tennis was clearly secondary," said his mother. "We told him that whatever he wanted to do was OK. If he never played again, it would be OK with us; we just wanted him to be healthy and happy."

Here is the perspective Marco worked to achieve after the painful loss. It's the one we should all try to attain when the game deals us a rough hand:

- What happened to me was normal, predictable, and natural.
- It happened because I probably cared too much, because I wanted it too badly, not the opposite.
- It means I'm human and am willing to take big emotional risks with myself.
- It means I really care, and that's a big plus.
- What happened to me was not failure, but learning, necessary learning; not a step backward but a giant step forward toward greater self-understanding and mental toughness.
- The way I deal with the losses from here forward is far more important than the losses themselves.
- The meaning of this loss in terms of my career is probably next to nothing.
- I lost control of my game simply because I lost control of my biochemistry. The chemistry of fear became too dominant.
- I must and will learn how to control my emotions more skillfully.
- I'm eager to try again to keep the chemistry of my body fueled, not from fear but from fun, enjoyment, and challenge.
- I've learned a lot and am ready for the next one. Put me in, coach; I'm ready.

Marco's confidence began to return. Two weeks later, he met Daniel in the Lion's Den at the Nationals in Kalamazoo, Michigan. But this time

Tennis is capable of producing extremely high levels of competitive stress, as Thomas Muster demonstrates. Emotional control is the key to managing stress.

he slew the dragon. Inside. He reached the quarterfinals and, according to Marco, he played great.

"I just decided to go out and do my best and have fun," he said. "If I lost in the first round, it would have been OK, as long as I gave it my best shot."

Marco has a new respect for the punch of this game. To stay on top of it, you've got to do your homework. Strangely, it's the mental challenge that makes the game so great.

Third-Degree Burnout

Marco Cacopardo was able to work through his anxiety problem in just a few weeks. Other players haven't been as fortunate.

Howard Schoenfield was the epitome of success. In 1975, he won every junior tournament he played and was ranked No. 1 in the world in the boys' 18s. Everyone who saw him play said virtually the same thing: he was destined to become a great player, he had it all. Despite his fame and the promise of greatness, however, Howard quit the game, didn't touch a racket for nine years, and underwent a prolonged period of emotional conflict, confusion, and personal doubt. "The pressure proved too much," he recalls. "I couldn't take it. All the fun and excitement were gone." To help parents and kids deal with the pressures of junior tennis today, Howard, now back in the game as a coach, gave the following interview:

Considering your background and experience, how much pressure do you think junior tennis exerts on kids?

The pressure can be devastating.

Where does it come from?

I think most of the pressure comes from the money involved. But, more than that, it comes from the people involved in the game itself.

How much was junior tennis part of your difficulties while growing up?

The pressure of tennis was a major part, but I didn't have an escape mechanism. I had no one to turn to. There was no way to blow off steam, no one to say, "Hey, this is a game." The pressures of junior tennis build and build, and you need someone or something to bring you back. Let's look at the long term: This is a silly little game. In terms of life and death, it's pretty insignificant. When it comes to being a good person, feeling good about yourself, feeling good about life, those are the things that are important. How do you feel inside about yourself? What's your own self-worth or self-esteem?

You were the No. 1 junior in the world in 1975. You won every tournament you played. Was that the year you felt the most pressure?

Yes, because I was expected to [win] all the time, to continue performing at that level. That kind of pressure can be so immense if you don't have support, if your own makeup is such that you can't deal with the pressure, if you can't put the whole thing into perspective. Hitting the ball on the tennis court isn't the most important thing in your life, but you can start feeling like it is. You're the same person when you walk on or off the court, win or lose. Your personality should not be on the line every time you walk out there.

Did your self-esteem get totally connected with the tennis court?

There was nothing else. I was what I was because of what I did on the court. When I walked on the court, that was me. If I lost, I wasn't anybody.

How do we avoid letting that happen?

You let the kid know you love him—win or lose. "You are the same person. I love you. I care for you the same way—nothing changes." If the parents don't understand that, the kid is going to be very frustrated. He's going to be afraid. How many times do you throw up before a match because you are afraid? It can get so out of perspective. The parents' role has to be one *with the kid.* Don't let the kid's whole life depend on hitting yellow balls over a net. Parents and coaches sometimes believe that no one can really get hurt emotionally by this game. Oh, my God, there are scars everywhere you turn. I mean, talking later in life, it took me nine years.

What about parents?

I think 99 percent of the parents really want to help. No parent wants to screw up his kid. They know there is pressure at every level of the game—a kid playing at a local club in front of parents, a kid playing at the state level. Is the pressure greater playing in your first tournament at the club or at Kalamazoo [Michigan, site of the USTA Nationals]? I don't know. A kid playing his first tournament, with parents and friends watching, experiences great pressure. The parents want to be good tennis parents. But you aren't born with it, you have to work on it.

Even if a kid never plays tennis, he's going to have problems. Through your twenties and thirties, sometimes you have emotional or personal problems to deal with. This game amplifies them and gives added pressure. If things aren't right, you can crumble a kid, you can break him. Parents think, "This can't happen." Those are the ones who better open their eyes and look. It can happen to anyone.

Can a coach be a bad guy sometimes, yet not quite as devastating as a parent?

A lot of times the coach has to be a bad guy. You can be a friend to a child to an extent. You have to respect and trust him, but you can't get too close—you've got to hold the reins. You can't choke the kid. Keep perspective on what's important and not important. Keep in mind that this kid's life is the most important. Is he having fun? Because these are the years he can't get back—never. Obviously, you can never go back. We never really know how tough this game can be until all of a sudden we have all these kids just falling out. This game can be absolutely devastating.

What should be the parents' role in the game?

A parent's role has to be one of support more than coaching. I think once a parent departs from this, the problems start; and as a tennis player grows in experience, the problems grow with it. I think there are very few instances where you can have that "close" relationship as a parent and also have a relationship as a coach or mentor.

The parents have parental duties: the caring, loving, and discipline that a normal parent-child relationship needs to succeed. If a child needs to be disciplined for bad on-court behavior, then the coach ought to take steps to discipline the child in that manner, but this is not saying that the parent can't discipline the child for not picking up his room and things like that. This is normal parental activity. But once a parent tries to move into tennis discipline, he becomes a bad guy in the tennis atmosphere and that creates a lot of pressure for the child, because the child has nowhere to turn. I think a parent has to be very supportive of the tennis. His main concern should be, "Is the child having fun?" because once this game stops being fun, it's over. It's over for the child, over for the player.

Do you think the pressure was much different when you were a youngster than now?

I think it's greater now. People see big dollars at the end of the tunnel. They don't realize that there's a small percentage of people who are going to obtain those kinds of goods at the end. It's just about impossible. Why ruin an individual trying to achieve percentages that are so low? Instead of looking at what my son or daughter can achieve, shouldn't I concern myself with whether that individual is happy with himself, is he having fun?

If you had to write a story on what effect junior tennis had on your life, how would you write that story?

I wouldn't write it negatively. It's a great game, a great sport. My problems were brought about by me and my circumstances. At the same time, other people came through unscathed, had great careers and a lot of fun. I enjoy playing the game at certain times now, and I enjoy being associated with it again.

Stress: The Vital Statistics

We've read of two cases where stress drove talented players away from the game for a period of time. Are the stresses of junior tennis always bad? Where does the stress come from? What are the consequences? Who is likely to be victimized?

In tackling these tough questions, it's important to understand that physical training represents controlled doses of physical stress that lead to higher levels of fitness, strength, and agility. Emotional training, something I like to refer to as mental-toughness training, involves controlled doses of emotional stress leading to better emotional strength, control, and fitness. A typical practice session of drilling, hitting two-on-one, line running, and so forth is essentially physical stress. A tournament, however, creates both physical and emotional stress.

Controlled doses of stress are acceptable as long as the stress is manageable. Too much physical stress is linked to injury, fatigue, a breakdown of physical skills, and, ironically, a wide range of emotional problems. Too much emotional stress is linked to emotional breakdown, which at its extreme is called burnout. Problems of attitude, motivation, confidence, moodiness, and depression are common consequences of excessive emotional stress. Too much emotional stress also has been linked to increased risk of injury and depressed immune system, which decreases the body's ability to ward off infection and disease.

Emotional stress is a biochemical response at the most basic level. Stress is not an external event. Contrary to what most people think, it is not the bad line call, the wind, or the tournament itself that is stressful. Rather, it is one's biochemical response to the event that determines stress levels, and that is determined by how you perceive the event. If you perceive the event as threatening, it is likely to be very stressful. If you perceive it as enjoyable, little stress will be produced.

Parents and coaches need to grasp two important concepts. The first is that an integral part of emotional training is exposing young players to new and therefore potentially threatening events. Teach them how to perceive and respond to them so that stress hormones are not dramatically triggered. The second is that the emotional cost of an event for a child can be determined by the degree of nervousness, anger, fear, depression, and negative or self-critical behavior. The same event may be extremely stressful for one child, while not at all for another.

What is burnout? Plain and simple, burnout is the consequence of excessive stress, either physical or emotional. Working too long and too hard physically, or feeling too much psychological pressure for too long, will produce burnout. For example, playing too many tournaments in a row can frequently lead to *temporary* burnout; too many tournaments, too much pressure, for too many years can lead to *permanent* burnout.

Burnout studies indicate that the effects occur in progressive stages. In stage one, the child's sense of enthusiasm and energy begin to decline. Young players show more fatigue and irritability than usual. The early physical signs typically include complaints about upset stomachs, minor body aches, and headaches. Eating too much or too little is often associated with stage one.

Stage two is characterized by two dominant themes: withdrawal and anger. The result is a decline in self-esteem, energy level, and overall enjoyment of the game. Prolonged colds and flu, severe fatigue, sleep difficulties, and sudden weight gain or loss are common physical symptoms.

The third stage of burnout is a pervasive loss of confidence and self-esteem accompanied by feelings of intense depression, alienation, and withdrawal. At this stage, players have virtually no energy, no enthusiasm, and have real difficulty verbalizing what's happening to them.

Some children are clearly more vulnerable, and therefore at higher risk, than others. Youngsters who suffer burnout often manifest similar personality characteristics. Kids most vulnerable fit the following profile: highly motivated, perfectionistic, and often overachieving; strongly influenced by powerful "oughts" and "shoulds"; have a great need to be liked; extremely sensitive to criticism.

Ironically, these are often the same kids coaches love to work with. They are eager to please, never talk back, and are highly motivated.

Kids who leave home to attend full-time tennis academies face greater stress challenges. For the last 18 months, data has been collected contrasting stress levels of three separate groups: full-time academy students living away from home; academy students living at home (day students); and non-academy students living at home and working with a local pro. Of the three, the full-time academy students experience the greatest stress due to the lack of personal freedom, privacy, personal time, personal coaching, and non-tennis activities. Non-academy students working with a local pro experience less stress than full-time academy students, but more than day students. For them the greatest stressors are tennis-related: scarcity of good people to play with, lack of progress, low confidence, and overall performance. The group living at home but attending an academy experiences the least stress. These juniors' greatest stress factor is insufficient time to play.

Although full-time academy life is the most emotionally challenging, many kids seem to thrive in this environment. From my experience, the kid who handles stress well fits a particular profile: 14 to 17 years old; highly motivated; independent and self-directed; sets lofty but realistic

Catherine Tanvier turned pro at 15. Although teenage girls can compete successfully on the women's professional circuit, it poses great challenges.

goals; hard-working and disciplined; can say no and often is assertive; gets along well with peers but is not overly concerned about being liked; emotionally stable (not prone to moodiness or depression); has parents who are supportive but not pushy; has sound fundamentals.

10 TIPS FOR MANAGING JUNIOR STRESS

1 Be careful not to overtrain physically; know when enough is enough.

2 Practice for short periods of time with high intensity. Several short, intense practice periods are better.

3 Think of the time off between practice sessions or matches as part of your training. Relaxation and recovery are as important as work.

4 Don't play too many tournaments in a row. Resting between bouts of emotional and physical stress is extremely important.

5 Know your stress signals. Monitor your gauge of stress buildup. Low energy, moodiness, loss of sense of humor, sleep problems, persistent colds, or pains are good gauges.

6 Learn to say no. Let people know when you've had enough.

7 Work to view tennis matches as challenges, not threats. Remember, situations are not anxious or stressful—people are. It's your perception of the bad line call, or of losing to someone you shouldn't, that triggers the stress chemicals.

8 Track your stress levels daily. Make a chart and rate your physical and emotional stress levels on a scale from 1 to 10. The closer to 10 in either category, the more important it is to relax.

9 Try new and creative things in training. Boredom is also stressful.

10 Don't postpone your happiness until that special goal is achieved. If today was the last day you could ever play tennis, ask yourself, was it worth it? If the answer is no, something is wrong.

Parents—Powerful Positive Motivators

What is the parent's role in creating and preventing junior stress? And what can mothers and fathers do to best ensure their child's success and happiness in the game?

Parents can put their child on the road to success in tennis by stimulating interest and enthusiasm for the game early in the child's development. According to studies conducted by researchers Gian and Chander Sahota, parents who spend a lot of time with their kids in the beginning stages of tennis—having fun, hitting balls, playing silly games—are planting the seeds for high achievement. By investing time and having fun themselves, the mother and father serve as powerful positive motivators.

The most important role for parents is to light the fire of achievement. It is done most effectively by creating an atmosphere of enjoyment. Once the fire has been lit, the parents' role must take a new direction. If they remain too close, they start smothering the flame. Motivation must now be generated by the youngster's peers and coaches, and from within. The parents' new role is simply to be supporters—from a distance.

Some children tend to be more stress-prone on the court. Such highly anxious children have the least chance for experiencing high achievement. They often become victims of the competitive world of junior tennis. As a rule, a child with the high-anxiety trait will have less fun in competition, experience less competitive success, and run a higher risk of burnout.

To reach a high level in tennis you must reduce this anxiousness. As one might expect, parents play the most powerful role in the development of the high-anxiety trait. For this reason, parents need to examine the things they do that foster this tendency.

Research has identified four parental practices that are tied to the learning of this trait. First, parents who tend to rely on the use of fear, punishment, or the withdrawal of love increase the likelihood that their children will manifest the high-anxiety trait. Second, generally, the more intense the punishment, the more likely the high-anxiety trait will develop. Third, inconsistent parental practices make the child feel uncertain and fearful of how to control situations. An example in tennis would be telling your child before a match that effort and attitude is everything, and then proceed during and after the match to respond in ways that clearly indicate winning is more important. Fourth, restrictive parenting limits a child's opportunities to cope with new and different situations. In tennis, the longer the list of *can'ts* imposed by parents—you can't play with that person, or at that club, or in that tournament, or you can't play unless you practice in this way or under these circumstances—the more problematic anxiety becomes.

In other research it was found that parents of high-anxiety children were: more likely to withhold reward or praise when their children performed correctly; more apt to show negative expressions of tension or irritation; less likely to show positive emotion and enthusiasm; and less apt to respond to expressions of insecurity.

Undoubtedly, parents have the power to shape the success and failure of their offspring's future.

PARENTAL DISCRETION

- Make sure your child has fun playing tennis. Spend as much time as you can playing silly games, laughing, and enjoying the sport. If you don't know how to play tennis, learn by hitting balls together.

- De-emphasize the importance of competitive success and emphasize the importance of fun and effort. Be very sensitive to the response of fear or threat by your child. If competition is threatening, stay away from it until the child is ready and eager.

- Once you've successfully planted the tennis seed, and your child is motivationally strong and advancing in skill development, start removing yourself from the picture.

- Don't use fear or punishment to get your child to do the things you think he should do in the game. Except in the case of cheating or unsportsmanlike behavior, at all times exhibit positive emotion.

- Be consistent. Don't say one thing and then do another. And don't let your own needs influence your child's development.

Adult Situations

We've read about the emotional pressures and stress associated with junior tennis. But issues of stress, burnout, and overtraining apply to adults as well. Even at the highest levels of adult tennis, controlling stress is a major factor in performance success. Ask Martina Navratilova. Before Wimbledon in 1987, Martina had not won a tournament all year. The French Open final had been particularly stressful. Serving for the title at 5-4 in the third set against Steffi Graf, two consecutive double faults confirmed that Navratilova was human after all.

Stress is an inevitable consequence of being out there, going for it. The secret is controlling stress, not eliminating it. The only way to completely eliminate stress from competitive tennis is to quit. The only real solution is increasing self-control.

When stress levels become too high, just as in junior tennis, the risk of burnout, injury, and poor performance dramatically increases. Learn-

Herb and Aaron Krickstein consult. Parents light the fire of achievement by creating an atmosphere of enjoyment and support.

ing to better manage the stress associated with competitive tennis requires self-understanding. The following two questions often provide important insights.

Question No. 1—*How stressful is this match I'm about to play?*

To help answer this question, mark the following five items and total your score.

1 Your level of motivation for this match. 1 (low) 2 3 4 5 (high) The higher your motivation, the greater the potential stress.

2 Your level of confidence for this match. 1 (high) 2 3 4 5 (low) The lower your confidence level, the greater the potential risk.

3 How important this match is to you. 1 (low) 2 3 4 5 (high) The more importance you place on the match, the greater the potential stress.

4 How much of a catastrophe it would be if you lost or performed badly in this match. 1 (minor) 2 3 4 5 (major) The greater the potential catastrophe in your eyes, the greater the potential stress.

5 How sensitive (nervous) you typically get in your competitive matches. 1 (low) 2 3 4 5 (high) Anxious, high-competitive-trait individuals are at greater risk.

Add the numbers you circled for each of the items. If your total is 18 or more, the match needs your special attention from an emotional training perspective. Unless you emotionally prepare for this match in the right way, stress levels will likely be very high.

Question No. 2—*How stressful was the match?*

To help answer this question, mark the following six items and total your score.

1 Your level of nervousness during the match. 1 (low) 2 3 4 5 (high)

2 Your level of anger and frustration during the match. 1 (low) 2 3 4 5 (high)

3 Your level of embarrassment during the match. 1 (low) 2 3 4 5 (high)

4 How nervous and tight you were before the match (pre-match anxiety). 1 (low) 2 3 4 5 (high)

5 How depressed and upset you were after the match (post-match depression). 1 (low) 2 3 4 5 (high)

6 How much fun or enjoyment you had during the match (note: the scale is reversed). 1 (high) 2 3 4 5 (low) The more fun, the less stress.

Add the numbers you circled for each of the items. If your score is 24 or more, the match was very stressful.

Just as with young players, the signs of excessive stress for adults include depression, loss of concentration, moodiness, low energy, low enthusiasm, boredom, and lack of fun.

Scientific studies show that adrenaline flow corresponds to the level of stress. Sports like tennis that require precise concentration, delicate motor control, and balance necessitate adrenaline levels that are only slightly above normal resting rates. We are all familiar with the dreaded "adrenaline rush" just before a big point or game. This mass discharge of adrenaline for tennis players nearly always translates into the "choking response" and tight, uncoordinated play.

What does adrenaline do? It actually prepares the body for short, sudden bursts of intense activity. Dramatic increases in adrenaline make you stronger and increase your endurance, but your ability to control motor skills and maintain a moment-to-moment intense concentration decreases. Blood flow to the heart and vital organs increases while flow to the hands and feet declines. Most tennis players report that their feet start feeling heavy and slow, their hands loose. As blood flow is diverted away from the limbs to the skeletal and heart muscles, hitting the tough returns and passing shots or volleys becomes increasingly difficult. The pounding heart rate, rigid muscles, and soaring blood pressure mean you've become too angry, too nervous, too intimidated. Your adrenaline levels are too high; the stress too much. The "Becker Boogie," the "Connors Stoke," the clenched fist of a Lendl or Navratilova after a great shot are adrenaline-stimulating behaviors. Although the biochemical mechanism is still unclear, strong positive emotion often produces a state of high energy arousal without accompanying disruption of motor skills and concentration.

Researchers David Glass and Jerome Singer gave two groups of people a number of mental problems requiring good concentration while exposing them to very loud and unpleasant noises. One group was not told of any way it could stop the noise. The other group was told it could stop the noise by pushing a button but the tester preferred the subjects not use it. The second group had the feeling of control over the noise stress even though they still endured the same noise level. That simple feeling of control enabled the second group to perform significantly better than the first group.

Between the 1987 French and Wimbledon championships, Navratilova seemed to renew her self-belief and her ability to handle the stress of competitive play. Facing the same opponent in the Wimbledon final she had lost to in the French, she appeared emotionally prepared the second time around. The turning point was Martina's refusal to get upset after losing six set points in the first set. Each time one slipped away, she simply went back and took control again. On the seventh set point Navratilova prevailed.

STRESS-CONTROL FORMULA

These six steps can improve your stress control skills for match play:

1 Make a firm commitment in writing to improve your emotional control/ stress-management skills during the next six months.

2 Prior to each match, estimate your anticipated stress factors using the items in Question No. 1 described earlier.

3 Set match goals for how you intend to perform emotionally during play. Be specific.

4 Rehearse physically and emotionally how you intend to respond when things get tough.

5 After each match, calculate how stressful the match was for you using the items in Question No. 2 described earlier.

6 Grade yourself on your emotional performance.

You'll know you're on the right track when you start feeling the "three Cs" as the stress starts to mount: *Control,* able to balance relaxation with energy; *Challenged,* able to keep positive emotions engaged; *Commitment,* able to generate great intensity and effort and still maintain control.

Questions and Answers

If my mail's any indication, controlling nerves and stress is the player's greatest concern in the mental game of tennis. Following are some of the questions people have asked me in this area.

Q *My daughter is a top 14-and-under competitor in our section but she tends to be a worrier. She's played tournament tennis since she was 10. The question I have concerns the way competitive tennis affects her health. Is it common for kids to get colds and the flu around tournament time? My daughter constantly gets sick when she plays tournaments. For a long time I thought she made it happen so she had an excuse if she didn't play well. I no longer think that is the reason. What can we do to help?*

A The real issue here is the effect of your daughter's stress hormones on her immune system. The level of certain hormones, particularly cortisol and catecholamines, can diminish the effectiveness of the body's natural defenses by altering antibody and natural cell activity.

Issues of stress, burnout, and overtraining apply to adults—even pros such as Mats Wilander—as well as juniors.

Today there is evidence linking life stress with immune system deficiency and resistance to illness. The mental stress your daughter experiences around tournament time is connected to her hypothalamus. Medical science has discovered a rich network of blood vessels that connect the brain's hypothalamus to the pituitary, the body's master gland, which stimulates the release of adrenal stress hormones.

For years immunologists thought stress hormones negatively impacted the effectiveness of immune systems. But it wasn't until advances in radio-immunoassay techniques that the impact could be directly measured.

If your daughter is a worrier, tournaments are probably highly stressful for her. But stress management techniques may help her control repeated colds and flu. I would recommend the following:

- Plan your daughter's tournament schedule carefully. Don't schedule too many tournaments in a row and avoid tournaments during highly stressful times.

- Be sure she gets plenty of sleep and eats well before, during, and after tournaments.

- Reduce parental pressure to win and provide a strong positive support system during tournaments.

- Have your daughter practice various relaxation techniques such as deep breathing, progressive relaxation, and meditation to help reduce stress levels.

- Have your daughter monitor her stress levels by keeping a written log of how she feels around tournament times. Set specific goals to control stress better and be more positive. Also, keep a record of how often and when she gets sick. Remember, the more fun she has at tournaments, the lower the level of her stress hormones.

- It's a good idea that your daughter have a thorough examination by your physician to rule out any specific medical problems.

Q *My daughter Cindy is 16 years old and whether she's on or off the court, she interprets the slightest setback as a major catastrophe. When things go badly off the court she can get depressed for days, then suddenly snap out of it and be fine. When things go badly on the court she acts negatively and stops trying altogether. The smallest thing sets her off.*

My husband and I have discussed this many times with Cindy and on one occasion had her talk with the school counselor, but nothing has helped. Her negative attitude, which we noticed two years ago, interferes with her ability to succeed and makes her very unhappy. Is it just a stage she's going through?

A Cindy's tendency to magnify failure and read the worst into minor setbacks, both on and off the court, deserves your immediate attention. Exaggerating the importance of failure on court is typically reflective of self-confidence, self-esteem, and emotional control problems related to tennis. The part that concerns me is your daughter's tendency to magnify failure off the court. Her unhappiness and episodes of depression are clinical indicators that need professional attention. Cindy's problem may not dissolve without outside intervention. Although Cindy doesn't feel she has a problem, you should try to get her to be open to outside professional assistance. It will help her grow as a person and guide her toward greater personal happiness.

Q *If you examine the lion's share of the most successful juniors in the 14s, 16s, 18s, and even the pros, you invariably find at least one (if not two) overly involved, obsessive, pushy parents behind the scenes. This seems particularly true for American kids. Having normal, loving parents who aren't overly involved appears to work against young players. For kids to reach their full potential in the U.S., do they have to have "nutso" tennis parents?*

A The distinction between pushy parents and supportive parents is often a fine line. The world of competitive junior tennis at the highest level is so complex that youngsters without highly involved parents have little chance for success. In the best of cases, parents discover that for a five- to six-year period, a substantial part of their life is consumed in helping their children achieve competitive success.

Another consideration is motivation. Children from poorer, less affluent countries are often more driven to excel than kids in the U.S. Our nationally ranked kids generally come from affluent homes where the price tag for junior success is extremely high ($10,000 to $25,000 per year). Affluency tends to undermine drive, so the parents try to become the dominating motivational force. They keep the pressure on to achieve, and invent all kinds of strategies to keep their kids practicing. When parents show what might be considered a normal level of interest, the youngster fails to work hard or sacrifice enough to be successful at a national level. So what we often see at the top are kids who have parents pushing to keep them focused, dedicated, and disciplined. Such parents do everything they can to keep their kids from being seduced away from tennis and into normal teenage after-school pastimes. How many kids from affluent homes would freely choose to do sprints, Nautilus training, distance running, drilling, and practice for two to three hours every day after school as opposed to just hanging out with their friends?

An amazing number of these children get through the parent-pushing and become outstanding players, but many more just learn to hate the whole scene. And, even a few truly "nutso" parents have success. The question is, *At what cost?* There is a real price to be paid and often success leaves the young player feeling lost and confused. Are these parents going too far? Ask the child.

Q *I am a teaching pro who teaches her own child. I wonder how you feel about coaching your own kids. I am concerned that I put too much pressure on my daughter, as I tend to be tougher on her than my other students. We do get into arguments occasionally about her tennis, but she says she still wants me as her coach. I'm concerned that I may be undermining her love for the game. She is 13 and is ranked No. 3 in her age division in our state. The expense of hiring another coach to work with her would be too much for our budget. What would you suggest to prevent future problems?*

A There are lots of teaching pros and coaches who inevitably end up having to work with their own children. This is risky, particularly as youngsters improve. In the beginning, the relationship is almost always beneficial. Most coaches are more critical—and harder—on their own kids than others. A teaching pro's children will typically get more pressure from the parent and will likely become more sensitive to that stress. When that happens, the child's chances for success diminish. It takes a very special parent and a very special child for the relationship to work. Your answers to the following questions are critical:

1 Do you have a strong, positive relationship with your child?

2 Does your daughter want you to coach her?

3 Do you show great patience with your daughter?

4 Do you support, praise, and listen to your daughter as often as you do the other kids you teach?

"Yes" answers to these reduce the risk. Discuss your fears, hesitations, and concerns openly with your daughter. Sensitivity, patience, and support are the cornerstones of a successful coach/parent role.

Dear Dr. Loehr:

You've never met me before but I hope you can help me. Right now I am so frustrated, angry, and confused I could die. I am 19 years old and just started my sophomore year at a top 20 college. My dream is to someday play professional tennis. I've had this dream since I was 9, but if things don't change soon, I know I'll never have a chance.

My tennis right now is terrible and has been for six months. The problem is complicated and involves my parents. They love me. They are supportive and caring. They strongly believe I will become a successful professional and, in fact, have devoted their entire lives to the realization of my dream. My dream has become their dream too.

They decided that no sacrifice was too great to help me become a success. During my last two years of high school my parents accompanied me to every high school match and all my tournaments throughout the United States. They even insisted on being with me when I went to various places for extra training. I have never been allowed to travel alone. When I went away to college, they moved to the same town so they could be sure I stayed on track.

My parents are very conservative and have a strong religious background. They're convinced I'm not strong enough to resist the many temptations of the world and insist they be there to keep me focused and strong. They feel I'm too immature and naive to handle day-to-day problems. They're against me dating or going out late with friends, and watch every step I take. They want me to have fun and do fun things, but always with the family and on their terms. My problem is simply that I can't stand it anymore. I want to be on my own, play tennis on my own, and go to school on my own. I want to choose my own friends and be my own person. I feel totally trapped. It's also terribly embarrassing having your parents follow you around all the time.

I have tried to discuss this with them several times but they always have an answer. If they weren't such kind, loving parents it would be easy for me to tell them to get out of my life. But every time I try to say how I really feel, I start feeling guilty. They'll do anything for me and only want the best for me, and my response is to hate them for it. That seems wrong, but I just want them to go away. I'm unhappy at school, unhappy with tennis—playing very badly—and feel terrible about myself. Sometimes I think I'll deliberately fail at school and tennis just so they'll listen. What kills me is that they never did this with my older sister. She turned out great, so why me?

I'm probably very immature, but I need to grow up sometime. It's maddening to have my parents over my shoulder every time I turn around. They've raised me well and I have strong morals. I really do feel I can make it on my own.

I'm suffocating and can't find an answer. Please respond as soon as possible with advice.

Very sincerely,

Lisa

Two days after writing this letter, Lisa had a long talk with her parents and told them she had sent me a letter asking for help. Four days after receiving Lisa's letter I received the following letter from Lisa's father.

Dear Dr. Loehr:

You have probably received a letter from our daughter, Lisa. We just had a long talk and she informed us of her letter to you asking for help. I'm certain Lisa must have painted a rather grim picture of us and before you respond to her plea for help, we wanted you to hear her parents' side.

Lisa's tennis is obviously important to us, but our greatest concern is Lisa's personal and moral development. The path that Lisa has chosen in life is very treacherous. She is 19 but very inexperienced and immature. She is a tremendous talent and we recognized this when she was very young. Lisa has dreamed of playing professional tennis for many years now, and my wife and I have devoted our lives the past few years to helping Lisa achieve her dream. God blessed us financially so that I could retire early and therefore travel full-time with Lisa to provide support, direction, and proper balance in her life as she pursues her tennis goals. It is our feeling that the pressure of competitive tennis combined with the challenges of adolescence and young adulthood are too much for many young boys and girls today. I'm certain you see this as clearly as we do. Without a strong, ongoing family and religious support system, Lisa's future would be placed in serious jeopardy. We would much rather Lisa quit tennis altogether than make the mistakes many of the young boys and girls make today.

We strongly feel we are doing the right thing, and hope you understand and support our position. Lisa is frustrated because she doesn't have the freedom most of her friends do, but deep inside, I'm certain she knows that we are doing what is best for her. She certainly knows that we are making such sacrifices only because we love her.

We pray you will understand and give our daughter sound advice.

Sincerely,

Lisa's father

After receiving this letter from Lisa's father I decided to speak by phone to Lisa (whose name has been changed) and her parents. Although I spoke to all three, my conversations with the parents and Lisa were separate.

The two letters clearly show how profound the conflict is between Lisa and her parents and how logical and rational each position is as viewed from within that particular perceptual set. In actuality, the conflict depicted in the two letters represents a common theme that frequently occurs in various forms in junior tennis. A summary of my telephone message to Lisa's parents is as follows:

As Lisa's parents, you openly admit she is immature and overly dependent. As long as you continue to treat your daughter as a dependent and immature child, she will continue to act like one. At 19, Lisa is a young adult, and the foundations for her morality and character development were formulated many years earlier. It is absolutely critical that you begin to allow your daughter greater personal freedom, responsibility, and independence. This applies to both her personal life and tennis life. What Lisa is pleading for is both normal and necessary for her growth as a fully functioning person. In spite of your insistence that you wish only to protect your daughter, your behavior in all likelihood stems from powerful dependency needs of your own. This scenario is particularly common with the youngest child in a family, as parents struggle to hold on as long as possible.

As is so often the case, Lisa's strivings for independence and self-autonomy are controlled essentially through feelings of guilt stemming from your willingness to sacrifice your life and happiness for hers. If things are not changed, Lisa's guilt will likely be replaced by strong feelings of anger, resentment, and even hatred toward you. Even more tragic, Lisa's passage into full adulthood may be permanently blocked.

A summary of my telephone message to Lisa is as follows:

Your frustration and anger are very understandable, but you must work very hard not to let these feelings undermine your school and tennis performance.

Telling your parents about your feelings and your letter to me was very important. It is critical that your parents continue to understand how you feel. Your independence and personal freedom must be negotiated through positive, strong communication. Ask your parents to allow you to travel occasionally to tournaments by yourself or with other friends they approve of. Once the new freedom is granted, make every effort to live up to the responsibility.

Another example of positive negotiation would be to persuade your parents to allow you to live by yourself during your junior and senior years of college. Another might be that they *not* attend your matches except in special cases.

Remember, if you allow yourself to become bitter, cold, negative, or insensitive in your communication with your parents, your negotiating ability will become seriously limited.

You are going to have some very challenging times ahead, but I am very encouraged by your letter and attitude. I believe the general direction of your conflict and struggle is constructive and potentially very positive. Be persistent, yet patient. Your tennis will improve as your feelings about yourself and your situation improve.

Chapter IV

WHEN THE
CHIPS ARE
DOWN:
REVERSING
A SETBACK

In my introduction I mentioned that David Hemery's study found that champions felt commitment and effort were the mental factors separating them from the rest of the field. Never are an athlete's determination and fortitude tested so thoroughly as when he suffers a setback, such as a slump or an injury.

In the case of a slump, the tennis player must carefully decide which aspects of his game to change and which to keep; whether he should play more or less; whether he should try new training or fitness exercises or stay with the old; and, perhaps most importantly, how to stay calm and wait out this frustrating phase in his career. An injury can be even more exasperating since, even if the player sustains a positive mental attitude, he still must wait for his body to cooperate physically.

In addition to emotional control, the support of the player's family, friends, and coach is crucial in successfully rebounding from a setback.

Riding the Comeback Trail

Tim Gullikson had been able to maintain a world ranking in the top 50 every year since he turned pro in May of 1975. At his best, he had beaten

McEnroe and Borg, and in 1979 he had attained a ranking of fifteenth in the world.

But in 1982—after dropping to No. 150, his worst ranking in nine years—32-year-old Tim Gullikson had serious doubts about his ability to compete with the best. "Nineteen eighty-two was the worst singles year I ever had," he said. "My ego was down on the floor and I felt terrible about myself. Once your ranking falls so low that you have to go through the qualifying, especially at my age, you can't help but wonder if it's over."

But suddenly, in 1983, Gullikson righted himself. His ranking rose to No. 34 the following year and his career was once again on track. He turned it around.

One of the big differences, according to Gullikson, between 1982 and previous years was that he started overanalyzing his game. "It was as if I no longer trusted myself to hit the ball well without thinking about it. I started analyzing everything and was constantly searching for a new mechanical change that would be the answer to get me back to playing well again."

Gullikson found that another major difference between winning and losing was his ability to manage mistakes. "In my best years, mistakes rarely bothered me. I'd make one and could go right on to the next point convinced that I would be successful. For whatever reason, in 1982 I found myself constantly getting upset at mistakes and was often unable to clear them from my mind before the next point.

"I started becoming increasingly negative and pessimistic, and all that kept mushrooming until I found myself not having any fun with tennis. I was playing matches and didn't even want to be there."

So, what enabled Gullikson to go from his personal worst to one of his best? And, more importantly, what can you learn from his travail?

According to Gullikson, four basic steps made the difference. The first was to become physically fitter and stronger. "I put myself on a regular training schedule that included sprint work, rope-jumping, agility drills, and aerobics," he explained. "I got a lot more disciplined about everything. I was also much more conscientious about my eating and drinking habits."

As Gullikson started feeling physically stronger and more disciplined, he found himself starting to feel mentally stronger as well.

The second crucial stage in Gullikson's transformation was becoming more relaxed on court. "I found myself constantly muscling the ball, particularly with my forehand. This was especially true on big points and when I got angry or frustrated. In my practices, I started focusing on keeping my muscles relaxed and free. I started tuning into tension levels and how they affected my play."

As with most athletes, Gullikson found that his breathing played an important role in staying relaxed. "Breathing out at contact point and taking deep breaths between points helped to keep the tension down. As soon as I started becoming more relaxed in my play, I started doing better."

The third step had to do with balance. "I started working on becoming more balanced when I hit the ball. I often found myself slightly out of balance while hitting, and that simply added more muscle tension. So I did a lot of drilling to keep my upper body very balanced, erect, and still during the hit. I also found that, for me, getting physically more balanced was directly tied to getting emotionally more balanced. When I was out of sync emotionally—angry or upset—it adversely affected my physical balance and tension levels."

The final amendment was to stop tinkering with the mechanics of his game. With the help of biomechanics expert Jack Groppel, Ph.D., once-and-for-all decisions were made about grips and his technique on strokes. "It finally dawned on me that I got to fifteenth in the world and hardly ever thought about mechanics. I played by instinct mostly, and somehow I lost that."

Gullikson didn't show tangible improvement for a full six months after implementing his four-step plan. "I began to wonder if my renewed effort and training was going to pay off," he recalls. "I can say for certain that if I hadn't made a commitment to stay with it for a definite period of time, I would quite likely still be floundering."

Slumps are an inevitable part of sport, and tennis is certainly no exception. When the reality of a slump hits you, remember Gullikson's turning points:

- Get in the best physical shape possible. Start a disciplined schedule of exercise and diet—now!
- Work on muscle relaxation. Deliberately train to reduce excessive muscle tension during play. Breath control can be very helpful here.
- Improve your balance. Work to maintain a better sense of physical and emotional balance during play.
- Avoid overanalyzing and constantly changing your strokes. If you've already lost your rhythm, more changes will add to your confusion.

Different Strokes

Tim Mayotte had a similar problem to Tim Gullikson's, but handled it in a much different way. Mayotte was determined in 1987 not to have the huge letdown he had had in 1986 following his dramatic, five-set Davis Cup quarterfinal victory over Leo Lavalle of Mexico. "It took months to recover and get my game back," Mayotte recalled. "I loved playing Davis Cup, but it really cost me."

However, the 1987 Davis Cup was even more emotionally traumatic for Mayotte. Two five-set losses in Hartford, Connecticut, one to Eric Jelen and the other to Boris Becker, plus the team loss to West Germany, were devastating. "I couldn't get rid of it," Mayotte said. "I felt so terribly disappointed in myself. I carried it like baggage around my neck. It was always there."

Mayotte also knew that if he didn't handle the losses better than the previous year, the rest of the season could again be a catastrophe. So he took only one week off after Hartford and played a special event in Vail, Colorado. He made it to the final, losing to Jimmy Connors in three sets. "Even though I got to the final, I felt emotionally fatigued and very uptight," he said. "I blew up several times on court, which I almost never do. The pressure of losing Davis Cup and of consciously trying not to play badly afterwards was still there."

After Vail, Mayotte lost to Joey Rive in three sets in the second round at Stratton Mountain, Vermont, the first round in Montreal to Kelly Evernden, and the second round of the U.S. Open to Mark Woodforde in five sets. And although Mayotte was pushing himself not to let the second half of the year slip away, it was happening. Self-imposed pressure in the early rounds and the chance to move up on the computer was inviting because of his poor performance in 1986. "The first set was always tight," he said of the pattern. "I couldn't settle down. I'd lose the first set, get my game going in the second and third sets, and then get tight at the end of the third and lose a close one."

After the Open, Mayotte lost to Robert Seguso in three sets in the first round at the Du Pont All-American exhibition at Amelia Island, Florida, lost in three sets to Jim Pugh in San Francisco, and to Jorge Lozano in the second round at Scottsdale, Arizona.

"That was it," he recalled. "After Scottsdale, I had had it. I couldn't sleep. I was at the end of my rope. I was ready to totally bag it. I was thinking seriously of taking four or five months off. It looked like the second half of the year was going to be as bad or worse than the previous one. All of my efforts not to repeat the nightmare of last year were failing."

Bill Drake, Mayotte's coach, was equally concerned. Drake seriously doubted that Mayotte should depart for Europe for six long, tough weeks in such a state of mind. But despite his own doubts and those of his coach, Mayotte decided to go. "I knew I needed to relax, to get the pressure off my back. What I needed was a vacation from the game."

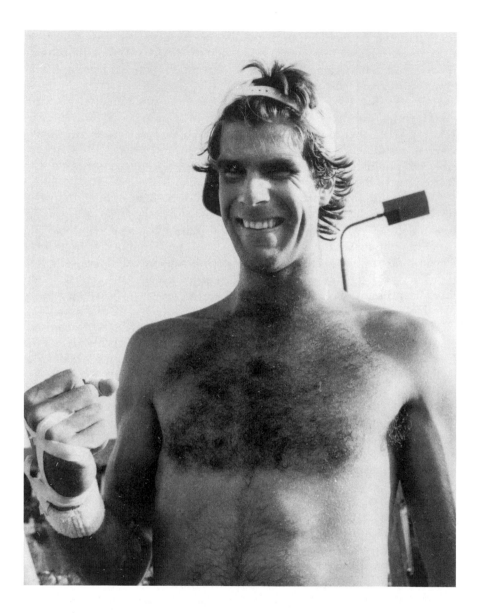

Balancing hard work with relaxation and fun proved to be the difference for Tim Mayotte. Learning how to relax and have fun was surprisingly difficult.

Mayotte made all his plans to go to Europe for the six-week tour and then the thought came to him: Why not make it a vacation? Remembering Connors' statement at Wimbledon, "I'm a guy on vacation in London playing a little tennis," Mayotte set out to enjoy Europe with his girlfriend, Cathy Barnett, and do all the things he'd always wanted to do. His attitude was, "I'll enjoy myself, practice very little, and play a match now and then." And that's what he did.

Mayotte virtually never practiced, ate and drank what he wanted, enjoyed sightseeing as he never could before because of his training schedule, and had Cathy (by her own admission an intermediate club player) warm him up before matches. "She's got a pretty decent forehand, and a weak, but improving, backhand," he said. For the entire European tour, Cathy's warmup became virtually Mayotte's only practice. For those who knew him well, nothing could have been more out of character. Perceived as a practice addict, his motto had always been "Prepare, prepare, prepare."

What happened from this vacation mentality was quite simply the best six-week performance in Mayotte's seven-year pro career. He started in Toulouse, France, seeded No. 1 with five full days of no practice before his first match, and won the tournament. In the weeks that followed, he made it to the quarterfinals of a tournament in Vienna, Austria, won the Paris Indoors, defeating Gilad Bloom, Slobodan Zivojinovic, Amos Mansdorf, and Brad Gilbert, and finished the tour with his first back-to-back championships by winning at Frankfurt, West Germany. Such a dramatic change from Mayotte's worst play to his best with virtually no practice: how could it happen?

For Tim Mayotte, the stress hormones started flowing prior to Davis Cup and continued pumping until the unusual European vacation reshuffled the deck. His answer to mounting stress and dwindling confidence in the past was always to practice harder, be more disciplined, make a better effort. But pushing harder is rarely the answer where too much stress is concerned. Mayotte's effort not to repeat the previous year's poor performance by *trying harder* is a common mistake; it only augments excessive physical or emotional stress. The answer lies in taking time off, relaxing, shutting down, getting away. That's precisely what Mayotte did. As soon as the pressure dynamics to win were reduced, his skills quickly returned. And it wasn't that he didn't feel pressure or nervousness at times in matches, because he did. The difference was the overall balance. When cumulative stress reaches a certain level, however, talent and skill mysteriously vanish. Only relaxation and recovery will bring them back.

We can all learn some valuable lessons from Mayotte's experience last year:

1   The solution to poor play when the pressure has been high is rarely trying harder. Trying harder simply perpetuates the stress cycle for many players. Ironically, the same attitudes that produce greatness—fighting spirit, determination, never-say-die—can also block it when the dynamics of pressure exceed a certain point.

2   Be careful not to overtrain before tournaments. Players often put so much effort and energy into playing practice matches, running, and training just prior to tournaments, that they arrive physically and emotionally stressed out.

3   Don't overtrain during tournaments. You may think you need to hit a thousand balls the day of your match to get ready, but you're probably better off relaxing.

4   If you have trouble managing tournament stress, make every effort to taper your training before you arrive at the tournament and try to do fun things other than tennis.

5   If it's likely that your poor tournament play is caused by too much pressure, set different match goals for yourself. By changing the expectations of what you should or shouldn't be able to achieve, the pressure dynamics change as well. Mayotte altered his goal from winning to having fun and enjoying himself, and that changed everything.

6   While at tournaments, plan your off-court time between matches with the same thoughtfulness that you apply to your on-court training. Schedule activities that will take your mind off tennis and also be relaxing and fun.

7   Try to reach your highest level of fitness prior to important tournaments. Tim worked very hard to get into top physical shape prior to Europe. Had his fitness been poor, the no-practice, no-workout strategy probably wouldn't have ended so positively.

8   Try to get those around you at your tournaments, such as parents and coaches, to understand that what you need now is not more pushing, more talking tennis, or more motivational speeches. Barnett understood how important her role was in helping Mayotte achieve a better balance of pressure, and she performed it admirably.

9   Think about what kinds of things reduce your particular pressure. Stress is very much an individual thing. What reduces your stress may be very different than what reduces someone else's. Your task is to focus on what you have to do to achieve a positive state of relaxation between matches, and then do it.

Reacting to Injuries

Research has shown that most slumps can be traced back to an injury. And once an athlete is injured, he is more prone to reinjury. Thousands of players each year navigate the dangerous waters of coming back from an injury. Players like Susan Mascarin. A top 100 player, Mascarin was successfully clawing her way out of the most devastating slump of her career. After mountains of hard work, she began winning regularly again. She reached the round of 16 at the 1984 U.S. Open and then the unthinkable happened. Mascarin turned her ankle before the match and was out of action for four months.

"It's not fair," she thought. "Why me! Why now! It can't be happening! It's the worst possible time!"

As Mascarin and any injured player will tell you, the physical pain of an injury is one thing, but the mental pain—the disappointment, frustration, anguish, uncertainty, and anger—is another. Ask any athlete working his or her way back through a difficult injury which was tougher, the physical or mental pain. It's generally no contest. Even more agonizing, long after the physical injury has healed, the psychological trauma can persist for months, sometimes years.

Surprisingly, I found that nearly three-fourths of all the athletes I see for slumps reported that an injury was associated with the slump's onset.

Injuries can have significant, long-lasting, negative psychological effects.

The thought of sustaining an acute injury, regardless of how temporary, takes on nightmarish proportions for most serious players. The most dreaded doctor's advice is: "Take a month or two off and see what happens." The chronic nagging injuries that never allow us to operate at full throttle constantly churn the waters of frustration until we find ourselves mentally broken. At this point, you might say to yourself: "I'm completely healthy now but I can't play! I've lost all my confidence." But don't give up. Here are some suggestions for reducing the psychologically traumatic effects of injuries:

- Acknowledge the mental battle and commit to winning it. Once you're out of action, realize that in addition to your physical battle you must fight a very important psychological one. Treat the injury as a crafty, stubborn opponent who doesn't play fair. You can allow your opponent to defeat you by turning negative, feeling sorry for yourself, and giving in to the depression. But you can also choose to fight. You can actually use the crisis to increase your mental

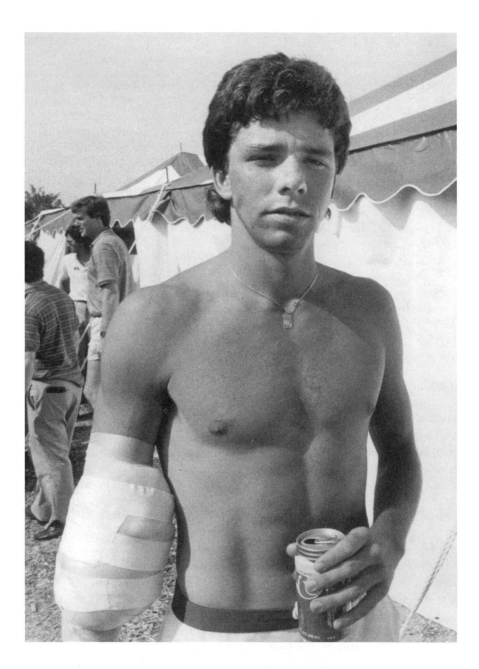

Injuries can have significant, long-lasting psychological effects, as they did for Jimmy Arias.

toughness, to get stronger mentally. You do that by staying positive, eager, and strong.

- Focus on accomplishing a set of positive goals during your rehabilitation period. The worst thing you can do with your spare time is to lay around. What you need is a new mental challenge, something you can get excited about. If you've always wanted to learn to use a computer, perhaps now's the time.

- Stay as physical as your injury will allow. Even though you can't play tennis, staying active is very important. It accomplishes two things: you stay physically fit and can return to full-speed play more quickly. Even more important, activity helps fight depression and negative emotion. If you can't run, can you walk? Can you bike, swim, do situps? Can you do Nautilus with your upper body if your knee or ankle isn't involved? Try to find something you can do, and do it regularly!

- Finally, keep a diary. Track your moods, your energy levels, what you're doing with your extra time. Record your mental ups and downs daily. It will help you stay focused and committed to your battle.

Injuries are inevitable in sports. They're part of the challenge. They actually offer opportunities to discover new possibilities. With the proper attitude, a forced layoff can be used to recharge your batteries, to keep you from burning out, and to gain a reflective understanding of your game and competitive style.

In the long run, it will likely be your *reaction* to your injuries rather than the injuries themselves that will have the greatest impact on your years of play.

Fighting Back

Injuries sometimes require more than just unwavering commitment and tireless effort. When a player is injured repeatedly, he needs courage. Courage to face the daily possibility of injury and to fight back against terrible odds. Courage is a trait often ascribed to military heroes and great navigators, seldom to teenage girls. In the case of Holly Lloyd of Deerfield, Illinois, the badge is well earned.

Lloyd began playing tennis at the age of 8 and had only one coach, Steve Casati, throughout most of her junior years. Casati remembers that Lloyd was very talented, but was even more impressed with how much fight there was in so small a girl.

"She was different, crazy about tennis," he recalled. "She was so eager that she couldn't get enough. Whenever I wanted to talk to her during a lesson, she would run to me at the net, and then write down everything she learned."

Unfortunately for Lloyd, her problems were about to begin, as her medical history illustrates:

October 1981. *Lost second round at National Indoors (seeded eighth), then discovered had pneumonia. Out until January '82.*

"I never should have pushed myself to play when I wasn't feeling well," Lloyd said of her showing at the indoors. "Then I came back too soon."

March '82. *Pulled hip muscle in exercise class. Out two months.*

May '82. *Sprained ankle. Out another month.*

Lloyd had just completed her first year of competition in the 12s, and she had very little to show for it. It was a year punctuated by injury, frustration, and heartache. Nevertheless, she was still highly motivated and began her second year in the 12s in good spirits, until the cycle began anew.

October '82. *After winning first-round match at the McDonald's Invitational in Lexington, Kentucky, Holly slumped down in pain. Later diagnosed as gastroenteritis.*

October '82. *Pulled stomach muscle. Out until mid-January.*

January '83. *Reinjured stomach. Out until April.*

April '83. *Contracted bad case of influenza. Withdrew from Easter Bowl. Out until June.*

By June, Lloyd hadn't played a tournament in eight months. She chose the Piseiffert Tournament in South Bend, Indiana, for the beginning of her comeback, only to lose in the third round to a local girl who had never beaten her before. Holly wasn't the same player anymore: where she had been confident and eager, she was now tentative and nervous.

"I could clearly see that Holly was very frightened," said Casati. "I told her to simply focus on being thankful she could play again."

Lloyd's first good tournament of the year was the National Clay Courts at the end of July. Unseeded, she got to the quarterfinals.

"Even though I did well at the clays," Holly said, "I started feeling like I had really let everyone down—my parents, Steve, and myself."

Martin Laurendeau knows that including periods of rest and recovery in your training cycle is critical to achieving peak performance.

In the last two years, Lloyd had missed four national championships, two Orange Bowls, five lesser national events, four local tournaments, and 11 months of practice. Although Lloyd and her coach worked on ridding her of her guilt and she went on to win the National 12s in August, her physical problems continued to intrude into her happiness.

July '84.   *After playing a full schedule the first six months of the year, developed flu at National 14 Clay Courts. Turned in quarterfinal performance, but forced to miss National 14s in August.*

September '84.   *Sustained painful lower-back injury. Out until February 85.*

This was the lowest point Holly, Steve, and her parents reached. By now, all had doubts about what the future held.

Holly: "I was more confused and upset than ever. Why me? Why do I deserve this? I'm doing everything I can to stay healthy and always breaking down. For the first time, I seriously thought about quitting."

Sandy and John Lloyd, Holly's parents: "We thought that maybe this was too much. Does she really need this? She's a great student. Maybe she should just focus on that."

Casati: "Holly started thinking that all her opponents were passing her by. The best girls were already thinking about turning pro. This was clearly the worst she had ever been."

After seven months off, it was now February '85, Lloyd's second year in the 14s. She had undergone physical therapy, massage, acupuncture, two cortisone shots, consultations with a half-dozen doctors, and a number of sessions with me. One of the most important discoveries made during this time was that she was highly allergic to many of the foods she was eating, specifically dairy products, sugar, and meat. To combat this problem Holly was put on a very restricted diet. She also began a weight-training program.

Her tournament performance that year was very inconsistent. She lost in the second round at the Easter Bowl, first round at the *Seventeen* Tournament of Champions, and round of 16 at the Clay Courts and Nationals. These were sandwiched around a victory in the Western Sectional Championships. Although she was physically healthy, she was still struggling.

The final breakthrough occurred in the fall of '85 when Holly decided to play high school tennis. She went undefeated for the year, made it to the finals of the state tournament, and played on the Chicago National City Team. She played her way back into shape, mentally and emotionally.

Periodic off-court training is necessary to achieve peak physical fitness for tennis. David Wheaton trains with his brother Mark.

There has been no looking back for Holly since then. After winning the St. Louis Invitational and making the finals of the National 16 Indoors, she played well through the summer of '86, ended up with a No. 3 national ranking in her first year in the 16s, and earned a berth on the Junior Wightman Cup team. Over the 1986 Thanksgiving weekend, Holly kicked off her second year in the 16s by playing up and winning the National 18 Indoors at the age of 15, a great triumph of will for one so young.

It took a great deal of inner strength for Holly to bring herself from the brink of hanging up her racket to winning a national championship. After winning the first battle of getting healthy through her restricted diet and weight-training program, Holly had to exorcise her own self-doubt. It turned out to be quite a learning experience for both coach and player, who offer this advice to anyone who finds himself or herself in a similar situation:

Holly: "Don't try to play when you're injured; pace yourself and don't overtrain; don't push to come back too soon from injuries; and, most important, look at the positive side of your injury. It gave me time to catch up on my studies, to improve my conditioning, and to get a new perspective on my game."

Casati: "When you take on the responsibility of coaching a young junior, you really take on much more than simply teaching her tennis. All her experiences teach her about life. And just because the kid is injured doesn't mean she doesn't need you. On the contrary, that's when she needs you the most.

"The single most important stabilizing factor in Holly's comeback," continued the coach, "was the unwavering support, understanding, and uncritical attitude of Holly's parents. Everyone stuck together. Without that, Holly would surely have given up the fight. Our commitment, from the start in '81, was based on friendship, and it grew stronger through all the adversity."

Chapter V

TRAINING STRATEGIES: PLANNING AHEAD

When Don Quixote said, "Forewarned forearmed," he wasn't kidding. Preparation is perhaps the most important key to mental toughness. As with any test of ability, there's no worse feeling than that of being unprepared for a tennis match. And, since match preparation is about the only thing you have full control over in tennis (other than your serve, which is still subject to the whims of the elements), you should take advantage of the opportunity.

In the past 10 years, scientists have developed a number of methods to mentally prepare yourself for competitive events. In the weeks and months before an important tournament, you can use training concepts such as periodization (a six-month training cycle that helps you peak competitively for a specific event); visualization (thinking in pictures to learn physical skills and control emotions); and working with the body's circadian rhythms. Then, the day of your match, use a mental checklist to help you relax, focus your mind, and adopt a positive attitude.

By preparing mentally well in advance of a tournament, then following a set routine before, during, and after each match, you'll train yourself to respond effectively to the challenges of competitive tennis.

Seasoning Your Game

For most players, the passing of winter heralds the coming of tournaments, league competition, and club championships. June, July, and August are the key performance months, when the most important matches take place. This is the period when you want your game to be at its best. The question is, how should you train now so that you will peak when you most want to?

A few years ago, I was intrigued to learn that several European countries, most notably West Germany, Czechoslovakia, the Soviet Union, Sweden, and France, were successfully applying a training concept called periodization to peak their players for important competitions. Although widely practiced in the United States in swimming, football, and weight lifting, the periodization model is generally unfamiliar to most tennis players and coaches. By contrast, some of the European countries have been applying periodization training to tennis players for more than seven years. The periodization model was actually first introduced in the Soviet Union by sports scientist L. P. Matveyev in the early 1970s.

Because of the reported success and enthusiastic endorsement of this training concept by several top European tennis coaches, a special group was formed to implement an experimental periodization program for a select group of 10 players enrolled at the Nick Bollettieri Tennis Academy in Bradenton, Florida. The planning and design group consisted of Ben Kibler, M.D., an orthopedic surgeon; Jeff Chandler, Ph.D., an exercise physiologist; Sergio Cruz, a former touring pro who trained in Czechoslovakia using the periodization system; and myself. The experimental program lasted from January to May 1988. The training objective was to get all 10 players to peak for late spring and summer competition. The competitive play of all 10 was carefully monitored throughout the summer. Eight of the 10 players improved dramatically, according to their self-reports and those of their coaches. The 2 that didn't improve failed to complete the entire training cycle due to schedule problems.

Periodization is a model for organizing the training activities of an athlete so that the chances of overtraining are minimized and the chances of achieving peak performance are optimized. The model seeks to organize five basic training principles according to specific phases: frequency—how often you train; duration—how long you train; intensity—how hard you train; variation—how much you vary your training; and specificity—how similar your training is to the actual demands of the sport. Periodization simply applies these training principles systematically to those areas of the body challenged by the sport. They typically include the aerobic system, the basic strength system, the speed and power systems, and the psychological or emotional system.

Applied to tennis, the periodization model would divide the training year into two complete training cycles of six months each. Although tennis has no off-season, you will have to decide when you want to peak and when you will rest and recover. Each six-month cycle will begin with rest from tennis and build toward peak performance. Your training routine will change according to five specific phases in the cycle: aerobic, preparation, basic strength, speed and power, and peaking.

The aerobic phase typically lasts from two to four weeks. During this time, players are encouraged to take a complete break from the game. No tennis! The training focus is cardiovascular and muscular endurance. Running, cycling, cross-training with other sports (such as basketball, soccer, and gymnastics) become the core of the training. The goal is to build a strong aerobic base as a first step. That means longer distances and slower repetitions, with 30 minutes of continuous activity four or five days a week considered minimal.

In the preparation phase, the primary focus is high-volume strength training, which results in a decrease in body fat and an increase in both muscle mass and short-term endurance. This phase typically lasts three to four weeks. Tennis training is non-competitive and focuses mainly on drill work, while endurance work is reduced from 30 to 15 minutes per day.

During the basic strength phase, the focus is on gaining strength in movements specific to tennis and laying the foundation for power and high-intensity work required in the speed and power phase. Tennis training during this three- to five-week period includes some competitive play and drills requiring speed and accuracy, but no tournaments yet. Endurance work is limited to one or two 30-minute intervals per week. Sprinting in one- to three-minute intervals is introduced on an every-other-day basis.

In the next three-week phase, significant gains in speed and power are generally realized. Weight training, running, and on-court tennis training emphasize explosive power and speed. Competitive play and drills simulating actual match play are the main training activities, but peak tournament performance is not likely to be achieved until the final phase. Distance running is limited to one 20-minute session per week and sprint work is introduced using 15- to 45-second intervals of maximum effort.

During the peaking and maintenance phase (which should be maintained throughout your prime competitive time), power, strength, and speed are peaked by reducing the volume and increasing the intensity of workouts. Training routines are as similar to the actual conditions of competition as possible. Endurance work is suspended and sprint work of 15- to 45-second duration is maintained until a few days prior to competition. The days immediately preceding competitions should be less demanding and stressful, both physically and emotionally.

So what does all this mean to the summer tournament player? How can periodization help you peak at critical times? Based on reports from other sports and those applying the periodization model to tennis, the following 10 tips should help your peaking efforts:

1   Arrange your tennis year into training cycles. Decide when you want to peak your game. If possible, divide your year into two complete cycles of six months each. The beginning of each cycle means a three- to five-week break from tennis, during which the primary emphasis will be on establishing a solid aerobic base. The last two months should fall at the most important performance time. Training according to specific cycles allows you better control of physical and emotional stress levels, thereby reducing risk of injuries, overtraining, fatigue, boredom, and burnout.

2   Set a target date to peak your game so that as the critical time approaches, you feel stronger and more eager.

3   Be careful about endurance work. Distance running and cycling should be completed by the beginning of the preparation phase and significantly reduced thereafter. Studies have shown that endurance training can limit gains in strength, speed, and power, particularly if the endurance and strength training is done concurrently.

4   Reduce your sprint and weight training greatly just prior to the peaking period. Limit your running to short distances at high intensity during the high performance period.

5   As tournament time nears, training should be similar to the actual demands of the game. That means less drilling and more set playing.

6   As competition time approaches, make the stress-recovery ratio of workouts as similar as possible to actual match play. The ratio is approximately 1-to-2: 10 to 20 seconds of high-intensity play followed by 20 to 30 seconds of recovery. Sprints, drills, and point-playing also should follow this ratio.

7   Remember: reducing your physical stress also reduces psychological stress. Increase your enjoyment of training prior to important periods, and follow routines that increase confidence and eagerness.

(above, left) Ann Grossman visualizes the perfect return during her serve return ritual. (below, left) Martin Laurendeau visualizes the perfect serve during his serve ritual.

8   If you haven't been doing any training or playing and have a tournament in three weeks, don't start doing everything at once and don't push extra-hard the first week to make up for lost time. Create a mini-training cycle that begins with low physical stress, builds to a peak in the third week, then tapers off just prior to competition. With only a short time to prepare, you're better off focusing most of your training on-court with drilling, point-playing and finally, playing sets. In the first week, play for shorter periods of time on a daily or twice-daily basis, if possible. Intensity should build from low to moderate by the end of the first week. The second and third weeks of training should consist of longer workout periods and build from moderate to high intensity. Just prior to the tournament, substantially reduce workloads and emotional stress levels.

9   A day or two before competitions, reduce your workloads.

10 Training in cycles requires more planning, discipline, and thoughtfulness than simply doing whatever comes to mind. But setting goals to peak at certain times and then planning your training activities accordingly will likely mean better performance, fewer injuries, and less stress—at the most important times.

Setting Your Competition Clock

The benefit of planning ahead and sticking to a routine is that it reduces the stress of feeling unprepared. All competitive athletes—from high school football players to professional tennis players—have regular practice times, set meals at set times, curfews, a quiet period before playing, and other rituals that relax the athlete and allow him to focus on the event at hand.

This type of rigid scheduling is especially helpful when you compete at different times of day or travel across time zones. This is when understanding circadian rhythms—internal clocks that guide your daily life—can be to your advantage. By stabilizing and adjusting your body's circadian rhythms, you'll have that much less to worry about before an important match.

The circadian phenomenon has been shown to affect more than 250 physiological and psychological functions, including coordination, balance, reaction time, memory, energy, arousal, alertness, and mood. Because of circadian rhythms, each person has energy highs and lows at roughly the same time each day.

Circadian patterns are regulated by an intriguing combination of internal and external factors such as sleep, food, stress, light, and social factors, and have a pronounced impact on psychological feeling states.

It's no accident that peak athletic performance generally occurs in mid to late afternoon. Circadian rhythms typically are at peak values in the late afternoon or evening and at weakest values between 3 and 6 A.M. No wonder most players dread the 8 A.M. match time. The probability of peak performance at that point in the circadian pattern is slim. And if you're a night person (owl) playing a morning person (lark), all the worse.

Circadian rhythms affect psychological feeling states such as moodiness, energy, alertness, vigor, and well-being, biochemically and hormonally. Concentrations of cortisol, epinephrine, and nonepinephrine, referred to as catecholamines, start to rise in the morning, peak in the late morning, decline just after lunch, and peak again in the late afternoon. A person's energy, alertness, and arousal correspond to this pattern. The same is true for the lark-owl differences. Early-morning larks secrete more epinephrine in the morning than in the evening; owls do just the opposite.

Higher levels of certain stress hormones have been associated with larks trying to perform in the evening and owls trying to perform in the early morning. According to one research study, trying to perform in a low-energy circadian cycle is equivalent to playing with little sleep or after consuming too much alcohol. The effects can be dramatic.

Understanding that changes in mood, energy, alertness, and vigor can be caused by changes in circadian rhythms is an important first step in gaining control. These changes, dictated by a rather precise system of biological clocks, often leave athletes feeling bewildered. "Why did I feel so lethargic?" they wonder. Knowing that such disruptive feelings can have a sound physiological basis, that it's not all in your head, can be reassuring.

Travel across time zones also complicates the athlete's task of understanding and controlling his or her biological clock. Jet lag is primarily caused by disruption of the circadian cycle. Travel across six time zones (as when traveling to Europe) can take more than one week for complete physiological and psychological readjustment.

Two issues concerning the circadian rhythm phenomenon must be addressed by tennis players. The first is stabilizing the cycles so the body is working in harmony with itself and capable of peak performance. The second is readjusting the cycles to allow for the various competitive demands of tennis, such as 8 A.M. matches and travel across time zones.

The most effective strategies for both stabilizing and readjusting the cycles involve careful regulation of the following factors: food intake, liquid intake, rest (nap and sleep schedule), workout schedule, social activities, and psychological stress levels. Stabilizing cycles is best accom-

Kevin Curren between points. Your mental and physical rituals between points play a major role in competitive success.

plished by routinizing schedules of meals, rest periods, workouts, sleep, etc. Athletes typically report that the more predictable (almost boring) their schedules, the better they perform. Readjusting or changing cycles is another matter. For instance, if you're an owl with an 8 A.M. match, following a combination of these procedures should prove helpful in resetting your biological clock:

- Eliminate your nap the day before your 8 A.M. match if you normally take naps in the afternoon.

- Schedule your evening meal the night before your match one to two hours earlier than normal.

- Try to go to sleep two hours earlier than normal.

- Get up in the morning a minimum of two to two-and-a-half hours before match time.

- Follow your normal breakfast and workout schedule prior to your match. Your pre-match workout is very important to resetting the cycle.

- Get yourself psyched up for playing the early-morning match. Thinking and acting negatively complicates the biochemical readjustment process.

Remember, the circadian rhythm phenomenon is real. Learning how to reset your biological clock and maintain it are necessary to achieve peak performance levels.

It's certainly worth your time.

Seeing Is Believing

One of the watchwords of the past 10 years, in tennis as well as other sports, is visualization. People often ask me, "What is visualization and do you think it can help me improve?" Here is my response:

Visualization simply refers to the process of creating images in your mind of past or future events, actions, or experiences. You think in pictures instead of words. Visualization generally involves a variety of senses, including visual, auditory, tactile, and kinesthetic, all of which serve to strengthen mental pictures. The practice of visualization has been used to accelerate the learning of physical skills and improve emotional control, concentration, self-confidence, and match preparation. In the strictest experimental sense, visualization remains a very controversial subject. For every good piece of research supporting its scientific use, there are an equal number of research articles providing no support.

The strongest rationale for using visualization as a training tool comes from reports by players. Most studies indicate that 80 to 85 percent of the top athletes consider visualization an asset in their training. From Greg Louganis to Bruce Jenner, Jack Nicklaus to O.J. Simpson, and Chris Evert to Martina Navratilova, visualization is perceived as vital to success.

The scientific rationale for using visualization as a training exercise stems from the fact that imagined actions activate the muscles similar to the way you actually perform the movement. Visualization can also cause powerful changes in emotion. It's important to understand that your brain can't distinguish between something that actually happens and something that's vividly imagined.

My personal experience with athletes supports the use of visualization to enhance performance. I've found that imagery practice builds positive expectancy for success and helps desensitize athletes to the frightening aspects of certain competitive situations.

VISUALIZATION ENHANCEMENT

Visualization is neither magic nor a panacea, but, if used properly, it can help you achieve your goals more quickly. "What you see is what you get" is more than a cliché.

There are several excellent books dealing with the application of visualization to sport performance. Here are a few tips to remember:

- Practice visualization regularly for short periods. Limit your practice sessions to 5 to 10 minutes.

- Practice when you're relaxed and calm. If you're uptight or rushed, you're probably wasting your time.

- Produce as much emotion and feeling as possible. Visualize in color, using all your senses, to simulate reality.

- Visualize things you want to change and see yourself as being completely successful.

- Use visualization as a tool for working constructively through potential problems or adversity prior to competition.

Your Mental Checklist

Many people feel better when they make "to do" lists: once something's in writing, you don't have to worry that you'll forget it, and it's always gratifying to check off a completed task. A tennis mental checklist can offer the same relief. It is a list of things to do before, during, and after a match to prepare yourself for the mental challenges that may crop up. Think about the situations you want to be prepared for, and add them to this list. A mental checklist should help you feel more relaxed and confident than ever.

The day before and the day of your match:

- The day before and the day of your match, follow very carefully your eating schedule. No candy or sugar-rich snacks; choose instead complex carbohydrates every two to three hours.

- Bring a towel to dry off on changeovers. Wear a water-resistant sunscreen on your face. Check your equipment—shoes, rackets, shirts, shorts—to assure that everything is in order.

- If possible, set aside 30 minutes before your match for quiet time. Use the time to prepare for how you want to feel and play during your match. First, get very relaxed and calm inside. Listening to soft, easy music is often helpful. Once you are relaxed, start rehearsing with mental pictures how you want to play and feel. Be sure to visualize situations that have given you trouble in the past, such as controlling your anger, staying positive, never giving up, and so forth.

- Hit before your match for at least 20 to 30 minutes.

- Get to your match at least 15 minutes early.

- Decide before you go on court what you will do if you win the toss—serve, receive, or choose the side.

- Use the full warmup time: hit plenty of forehands, backhands, serves, and volleys.

- Always bring a container of cool water to drink on warm days. Drink on every changeover. Fill a ball can with water if you don't have anything else.

- Even if you don't feel confident, energetic, or strong on court, *act as if you do!* By controlling how we look on the outside, we often can control how we feel on the inside. Act how you want to feel. You'll generally play your best when you can trigger a particular way of feeling inside yourself. The best combination of feelings is one of calmness, relaxation, high energy, and positiveness.

- Don't think about your strokes during matches—just play. The more you analyze, the worse you generally get. Try to think in pictures during play, rather than in words. The rule is: visualize during play, don't verbalize.

The racquet tells all. Derrick Rostagno.

- When you are nervous and not playing well, there is a tendency to start going too fast. Start slowing everything down: walk more slowly, don't run to pick up balls, take a deep breath before serving and returning, and take lots of time between first and second serves.

- To become a great player, you must learn to control your negative emotions. When things turn against you, don't panic, or become angry or upset. Rather, become challenged and inspired to turn things around and to break through the crisis. This is the most important step you can take toward becoming a mentally tough competitor.

- If you become obsessed with winning, you'll probably lose. Simply focus on doing the very best you can at every moment. Winning will take care of itself.

- Work hard to develop the reputation of being fair, honest, and a good sport. These are the earmarks of a real champion.

- Call the score out loudly before each game. When you're serving, call out the score before each point, especially during tiebreakers.

- Make your calls loudly and with confidence. If you are sure of your call, don't allow your opponent to intimidate you into changing it. Whenever you are not sure of a call, always rule in favor of your opponent.

- During your match, no whining, no excuses, no negative self-talk.

- If you feel your opponent is making bad calls, simply ask for a linesman rather than getting upset.

- Grade yourself immediately following your match on your emotional performance during play. Be tough on yourself here.

- Don't link winning with success and losing with failure. You may have experienced great success and still lost. Pair success with effort and learning. Ask yourself, Did I give my best effort, and did I do my best to be positive?

- The hardest part of competitive tennis is not learning the strokes, but rather learning to use your strokes under pressure. To become the best you can be, you must develop both physical and mental strength, and mental strength, because it's so much more intangible, is always the toughest. So every time you practice or play a match, work hard on the mental skills: staying relaxed, calm, positive, and energized.

If you want to ensure success for yourself as a tennis player, always *make it fun!*

Chapter VI

PLAYING
UNDER FIRE:
YOUR
ON-COURT
TACTICS

It may surprise you, but players with clearly defined rituals tend to hold up better under the pressure of match play than those without. Your service ritual may include tucking in your shirt, blowing on your hand, taking a deep breath, picturing a great serve, or bouncing the ball three times. From baseball to diving, from pistol shooting to gymnastics, such seemingly insignificant tics are indispensable to high-level performers.

Why are rituals helpful? Simply because they help us deal with pressure more effectively. As pressure builds during a match, we have a tendency to rush, to walk faster, to lose that natural sense of pace and rhythm. Strictly adhering to a well-defined set of rituals can significantly help prevent that from happening. Rituals help you deepen concentration, play more instinctively, stay relaxed, and raise intensity levels just before starting a point. They help keep your biological alarm from going off when things get rough and also help mobilize your mind and body for immediate, effective action. Religiously following a precise pattern of rituals should also mean fewer loose, sloppy points.

Many players are also surprised to learn that of the total time consumed in a match, approximately 25 percent is actually spent playing points. As much as 75 percent of the match is spent waiting to serve or return serve, or changing sides. Few players have seriously thought about training to improve their performance for that 75 percent. My experience has been that what you do during that time has a major impact on competitive success.

Reading Between the Points

Training to improve your performance between points centers on three primary objectives:

- Improving your ability to relax and recover between points; learning how to relax muscles, lower heart rate, and recover from the stress (both physical and emotional) generated during the point;
- Improving your ability to become properly energized and aroused prior to the start of the next point; learning how to generate energy and intensity from your positive emotions (the challenge response);
- Improving your ability to visualize and plan what you want to do on the next point; visualizing what you want to have happen, not what you don't want to happen (e.g., *Don't double-fault now!*) prior to the start of the point.

The following tips represent check points for improving your performance between points. Practice will make them automatic.

1   Eye control. Keep your eyes on your strings, the ground, or the ball to keep your attention focused between points.

2   Rituals. Establish rituals between and before points to appropriately balance relaxation, focus, and intensity.

3   Winning pace. Establish a winning pace between points, especially when angry, nervous, or fatigued, to regain emotional and physiological balance.

4   Breathing. Practice deep breathing between points to help relax and lower pulse rate. Breathe out at ball contact to get better control, relaxation, and feel.

5   High positive intensity. Even when you feel very fatigued or negative, project the image of having a high level of positive intensity. Fake it!

6   Calmness and relaxation. When nervous and tense, try to project the image of being relaxed and calm. Actively relax your muscles between points.

7 Negative self-talk. Avoid expressing negative self-talk during play. It only fosters bad results and pumps up your opponent.

8 Positive attitude. Think positively about your situation in the face of adversity. Become challenged.

9 Love the battle. Don't appear scared, threatened, or unhappy when things get tough; project a challenged and winning appearance at all times.

10 Racket up—"I'm up." Carry your racket in the opposite hand and keep it up, not dragging it low. This symbol says, "My racket is up, and so am I."

It's All in Your Racket Head

Most players never give a thought to how they carry their racket between points. Even fewer make any connection between racket-carrying habits and mental toughness.

The suggestion that the two are somehow connected often draws strange looks. But the next time you observe a match, pay special attention to what players do with their rackets between points. How do they carry them? Do they hold them by the handle or throat? Which hand do they typically use? Is the head of the racket up or down? Do they carry their racket differently when they win rather than lose a point? Can you read negative emotional states—anger, low energy, disappointment, carelessness, low confidence, negative thinking, and poor concentration—by the way the player carries his racket? The answer is generally "yes" with players who have mental toughness deficiencies.

Good competitors generally have excellent emotional control skills. Those skills are reflected in the way they walk, carry their head and shoulders, and yes, by the way they carry their rackets. The position of the racket can reveal a variety of negative emotional responses such as anger (when the dominant hand holds rigidly onto the handle like a club, with muscles bulging), low intensity, disappointment or no fight (racket head down, nearly touching the ground, carried by the handle with two or three fingers), and poor concentration (spinning the racket horizontally to the ground on one finger or carrying the racket casually on the shoulder hobo-style). Good competitors control their emotions and that's reflected in the way they carry their rackets. Between points, their rackets tend to project strong, positive emotions, regardless of the outcome of the point or game. Rackets held properly can project confidence, positive energy, and relaxation.

The emotional downfall for most players is mistakes. Mistakes can trigger strong emotional responses (disappointment, embarrassment, anger, temper, low intensity) that can cause inconsistent or poor play. For some players, nearly every mistake represents an emotional crisis. But it's interesting to note that everyone manages mistakes the same way when they're playing well. They simply turn and walk away confidently, as if nothing happened. Ideally, the best emotional response to mistakes is to get challenged. A mistake is simply feedback to the mental computer that the shot wasn't perfect, that some adjustment is necessary. And the simple fact is that without mistakes, the learning process would be permanently blocked. No mistakes, no progress. But negative emotion also blocks the progress and is a natural response to mistakes. So what's the answer? The answer is that players must train emotionally so that mistakes produce the right emotional response.

The typical sequence goes like this: a mistake will lead to an interfering emotional response such as anger. The player will express the anger (swear, throw his racket) by making more mistakes, and that's because the expression of anger is reinforcing in itself. It feels good to get it out. Once you throw your racket, the temptation to throw it again when you feel angry or frustrated increases. One of the best ways to break this emotional sequence is to act out how you want to feel following a mistake rather than how you actually feel. You act as if the mistake is no problem or as if you feel challenged and confident. The idea is simply to fake the response until you genuinely start producing the desired result. You act it out until it actually becomes a reconditioned emotional response. And the way you carry your racket plays a major role in this reconditioning process.

The 16-Second Cure

I've spent over 10 years gathering information—from personal interviews, videotape, and biofeedback instruments such as heart monitors—and analyzing what the world's top players do between points. From my studies, I've discovered that top competitors typically complete four rather distinct patterns of activity between points. Players with competitive problems, however, invariably fail to complete one or more of these activities. For training purposes, I've divided the patterns of activity into four separate stages and numbered them according to when they occur between points.

In Stage 1, the definable pattern of activity is a series of distinctly positive responses occurring immediately after the point, which seem to restimulate the flow of positive emotion. Stage 2 is a pattern of activity that appears to enhance the body's efforts to recover and relax from the stress of the previous point. Stage 3 is a mental pattern of activity that helps players continue to play intelligent tennis and to think clearly under pressure. Stage 4, which occurs just prior to the start of the next point, is a pattern of activity that assists the player's efforts to become focused and optimally ready to start the next point.

Top competitors learn these patterns through hundreds of hours of competition over numerous years. Studying the commonalities of the world's best competitors can help us develop a fundamental understanding of the mental and physical skills necessary for competitive success. Teaching these four stages enables players to learn mental toughness and competitive skills more directly and quickly. In detail, here's how the stages work.

Stage 1
The Positive Physical Response

Purpose: To facilitate the continuous flow of positive emotion or reduce the chance that anger, disappointment, or any other disruptive emotional response might interfere with playing the next point.

When stage starts: As soon as the point ends.

Length of stage: 3-5 seconds.

What you should do physically: Make a quick, decisive move with your body the *instant* the point ends. For example, if you won the point you might make a quick pumping action with your arm and closed fist. If your opponent made a great shot, you might clap using your hand and racket. If you lost the point, and this is the most important time, make a quick, decisive move away from the mistake as if to say with your body, "No problem." Immediately transfer your racket to the nondominant hand to facilitate blood flow and relaxation of the dominant hand. Hold it gently at the balance point between the handle and the head of the racket with the head slightly tilted up, projecting a strong, confident image. Never carry your racket by the handle with the head pointed downward, because it portrays a weak image. Both arms should be fully extended and hang freely at your sides to aid relaxation. Shoulders should be back, head up (chin level with the ground), eyes forward and down, projecting high energy; this produces a strong, highly competitive image.

What you should do mentally: You don't need to say anything, but if you do, follow these guidelines. If you lost the point due to a

Stage 1 Positive Physical Response

Stage 2 Relaxation Response

Stage 3 Preparation Response

David Wheaton demonstrates.

Stage 4 Ritual Response

mistake, say, "No problem," or "Let it go." If you lost the point due to your opponent's great shot, say, "Nice shot." This takes the pressure off you. If you won the point, say "Yes!" or "Come on!"

Stage 2
The Relaxation Response

Purpose: To allow your body to recover from the physical and emotional stress of the previous point and return your arousal level to an optimal range.

When stage starts: 3-5 seconds after the point ends.

Length of stage: 6-15 seconds.

What you should do physically: Continue your high-energy walk until you reach the baseline. Walk across the baseline and then slow down. Move back and forth across the back of the court. You can shake your hands out, stretch, spin the racket in your hand, bounce the ball on the strings, or towel off at the back of the court. Breathe as deeply and slowly as possible. Your eyes should be on the strings or on the ground. The important thing here is to keep your feet moving. Don't stand still waiting for the next point to start. Under high stress conditions, blood flow will pool in the feet and legs and slow you down if you stand still. Be certain not to walk right up to the baseline and begin the point. Always walk across the baseline. The more stressful the previous point or the more important the next point, the more time you should take in this stage.

What you should do mentally: Think only relaxing, calming thoughts such as, "Settle down, it's OK," or "Relax."

Stage 3
The Preparation Response

Purpose: To ensure you know the score and have thought about what you intend to do before the point starts.

When stage starts: As soon as you move toward the baseline to serve, or toward the return-of-serve position.

Length of stage: 3-5 seconds.

What you should do physically: After achieving recovery in Stage 2, move toward your serve or return position. If you're serving, stop about a foot or two from the baseline and pause. Verbalize the score out loud, looking directly at your opponent. Project the strongest, most confident and aggressive image possible. Notice David Wheaton in Figure 3, page 109. His image is strong and aggressive. His racket rests in his non-dominant hand tilted upward and he is blowing on his hand. This is the look and feel you want in this stage. The same is true on the service return. The receiver should project as powerful an image as possible, looking directly at the opponent as if to say, "I am confident I will win this point."

What you should do mentally: During this critical stage, consciously decide what you're going to do on this point. In a sense, you'll be programming the computer. Considering the situation and the score, ask yourself, "What should I do? Should I stay back, serve and volley, attack the second serve, play a long point, hit out, or return cross-court?" Consciously plot out what you intend to do on this point, either with words (e.g., "Get to net") or pictures (visualization).

Stage 4
The Automatic Ritual Response

Purpose: To achieve the highest state of mental and physical readiness prior to the start of the point. This sequence of automatic physical movements deepens concentration, balances intensity with appropriate muscle relaxation, and produces an instinctive, automatic form of play.

When stage starts: As soon as the player steps up to the baseline to the serve or return-of-serve position.

Length of stage: 5-8 seconds.

What you should do physically: For the server, two things have proven important—bouncing the ball a minimum of two to three times prior to the serve and pausing just after the last bounce. This pause seems to keep players from rushing their service motion under pressure. On the return, the ritual usually involves jumping up and down or swaying back and forth. Some players spin the racket; others blow on their hands. But your eyes should be fixed on the ball on the other side. The return ritual ends with a split-step, moving forward just prior to the server's contact with the ball.

What you should do mentally: Concentrate on your serve when serving, your return when returning. At this point, no thought should be given to technique, grips, or strategy. Most players benefit from a quick rehearsal of the serve or return that includes a clear image of where they want the ball to go. No self-talk is recommended during this stage.

It's important to note that if you miss the first serve, the same ritual sequence should be followed for the second serve. The time between first and second serves should typically last 5-7 seconds. Take a minimum of 16-18 seconds between points, not including second serves.

PRACTICE
MAKES PERFECT

- Following this four-stage routine will initially feel unnatural and forced, just like a new grip or stroke adjustment. With practice, however, this routine will begin to feel very natural.

- An excellent way to practice the sequence is to rehearse the stages on court without an opponent on the other side.

- Study videotapes of the top players going through the stages and videotape yourself in competition.

- While mastering the sequence, make your performance between points more important than your performance during points. Always strive for a perfect performance.

- For the pros, controlling their activity between points can be the extra edge in controlling a long match. It can make all the difference in your game too.

Rising to the Occasion

Between-point rituals help you recover from the previous point, relax, and direct your intensity on the next point. But often, despite consistent play, effective rituals, and overall mental toughness, people fall apart when playing the big points.

The ultimate victor in many matches is determined by the outcome of just a few key points. These big points, or pressure points, establish critical match momentum. Pressure dynamics and feelings of confidence markedly change in response to who wins the big points. Tiebreaker points, game points (especially break points), set points, and match points are generally acknowledged as the big ones. Good competitors consistently play the big-point situations well, while poor competitors consistently break down.

Many of the questions I am most often asked deal with big points. Typical are questions like, "Why do I break down on the big points?"; "Why can't I play the big points well?"; or "How can I play great until

As Gabriela Sabatini has improved the mechanics of her serve, her performance on
the big points has improved as well.

Steffi Graf rarely gets emotionally involved with bad calls. She simply turns and walks away.

the big points and then suddenly fall apart?" It's interesting that when I ask players why they play poorly on the big points, they all list the same reasons—poor concentration, no killer instinct, or no confidence. Such explanations rarely translate into constructive action.

The fact is that if you played well getting to the game, set, or match point and then suddenly proceeded to play badly, something changed for the worse. That's a breakdown. Players break down on the big points in any of five different areas: strokes, playing strategy, emotional response, physical response, or mental response.

Knowing specifically how you break down under the pressure of big points is the key to correcting it. Once you understand your faulty patterns and competition deficiencies, you can train to correct them.

Remember: if you didn't win but should have, something broke down. And for most players, breakdowns follow rather predictable patterns. Rather than responding with all-too-common but rarely productive self-criticism, self-directed anger, or guilt, pursue the question: what broke down? Take each of the five areas separately and gradually build a profile of how you typically respond under the pressure of big points.

Which strokes fail? The first question to ask following your match should be how your strokes held up on the big points. What strokes, if any, broke down on the big points or in pressure situations? Did your forehand, backhand, serve, or volley let you down when it was critical? Perhaps your approach shot or overhead smash failed as the pressure mounted. If, for instance, your forehand always seems to evaporate on the big points, in all likelihood it's not your head that needs fixing, it's the mechanics of your forehand. The biomechanics of all your strokes must be sound enough that you can still play reasonably aggressive tennis—even when you're nervous—without making too many unforced errors. Nervousness is actually a good test for the soundness of any given stroke.

And what about your second serve? If you tend to double-fault often on the big points, there's a red flag. Of all your strokes, your second serve is the most critical from a pressure perspective. Without a reliable second serve, one that can be hit with aggressiveness and depth under pressure, being tough on the big points is next to impossible. Players rarely connect match toughness with second-serve quality and consistency and, as a result, rarely practice second serves as a vehicle to improve their mental toughness.

The point is simply this: Players often attribute their poor play on the big points to mental factors, when in reality the real culprit may very well be a poorly designed stroke, where a slight increase in muscle tightness causes the stroke to collapse. If the same stroke consistently breaks down on the big points, make improving the mechanics of the stroke your number one training strategy for playing the big points better.

Where did your strategy go?   Many players believe they must do something very special and different on big points. As a consequence, players often break from the pattern and style of play that got them to the big point. Going for too much too early is a strategy breakdown. Going for the low-percentage winner is particularly tempting on the critical points (to get the high-pressure situation over with), but generally spells failure.

Another common way of breaking down strategywise on big points is to suddenly start pushing the ball back, hoping your opponent will make an error. Shifting to a very conservative, unaggressive style on the big points in order to keep your errors to an absolute minimum will be about as effective as going for too much too soon. The old dictum, never change a winning game, still holds. Whatever you did to get to the big point, continue doing. As a general rule, you will be most successful if you learn to play offensive, high-percentage tennis on critical points. You become the aggressor and work to get your opponent to make a forced error, without making an error *yourself*.

To do this, you must know your own game well. Your general strategy for big points should be worked out well in advance of your match. And breaking down is when you don't follow it!

Emotional Aftershock.   Players rarely have trouble being positive and energized emotionally on the big points. They know this is a critical time, so they generally give 100-percent effort and approach the point positively. So how do you break down emotionally on the big points? The breakdown actually occurs after the point is over, after the critical point has been lost. Becoming a good pressure-point player means you don't become overly angry, frustrated, or negative when you lose a big point. Losing an important break point often breaks the player emotionally too. The player fully realizes how important the particular point was and, from that point on, doesn't try as hard and is not as positive. And, in reality, this becomes the deciding factor in the match.

And what about choking? Being nervous on big points is not a breakdown. The fact is that players are likely to be nervous at critical times. The breakdown is determined not by the nervousness but by how the player responds to the nervousness in terms of strokes, strategy, negative emotion, and so forth.

How do you break down physically?   What you are looking for here are unproductive changes in your physical presence that may occur before, during, or after big points. The following questions reflect such changes: do you walk faster or take less time on big points? Do your eyes wander more on the big points, or do you keep your eyes riveted on the strings, ground, or ball between points? Do you stay with your normal pattern of rituals on the big points, such as bouncing the ball, tucking in your shirt, blowing on your hand before the point starts? How about your breathing? On the crucial points, does the pattern of your breathing change between or during points? Do you project a strong, confident, relaxed image on big points, regardless of how you actually feel? And if you lose a big point, do you suddenly look defeated, and let your head, racket, and shoulders drag?

Failure to perform consistently in any of these areas will clearly undermine your efforts to play the big points well. Breakdowns here, as in the other areas, follow rather predictable patterns. Deficiencies in these physical areas must be addressed before significant improvement in big-point play can occur.

How do you break down mentally? Players generally break down mentally in one of three ways. The first is that, because of their poor play on previous big points, they start thinking very negatively about the one they're currently playing. Examples of this kind of negative thinking include: "After losing three set points I can never win now," or "Here I go again, choking the big points away—I'm so bad."

The second breakdown area is negative self-talk. This is simply verbalizing outwardly your negative thought patterns. Verbally berating yourself for playing poorly on big points only makes things worse. Such negative self-talk can be a major block to playing big points well.

The third mental breakdown area is negative visualization. Players who have problems on big points are often the same ones who visualize just before they start the point what they don't want to have happen. They visualize not double-faulting, not hitting the ball into the net, not making a stupid error. And what they get is precisely what they feared— double faults, errors, etc. Those who play the big points well invariably have learned to picture as clearly and vividly as possible what they want to have happen before each point.

Remember, if you're not playing the big points well, something is breaking down. Understanding clearly how you're breaking down is the key to improvement. Begin by developing the most accurate profile you can of what typically happens to you under the pressure of the big points. Use all five breakdown areas to complete your profile. Then determine what you are going to do differently in your next match on the big points; create specific match goals. Being tough on the big points simply means eliminating breakdowns. Start working on your profile today and begin to turn your breakdowns into breakthroughs.

Handling Hot Calls

More disconcerting than big points for some players are questionable line calls. Let's go back to Wimbledon 1988 and a classic semifinal battle between Chris Evert and Martina Navratilova. The score is 5-6 in the third set with Evert serving at 30-40, match point number four. Navratilova approaches deep to Evert's forehand. Chris counters with a sharply angled cross-court passing shot, well beyond Martina's reach. Evert's shot, however, clips the top of the net, sending the ball dangerously close to the sideline. Evert, thinking the ball is good, turns away from the net and walks toward the deuce court. Navratilova, uncertain if the ball is in or out, anxiously turns to the linesman for a call. After a momentary pause, he signals out. Navratilova jumps into the air and lifts her arm in victory.

But the chair umpire remains silent. Is the match over? There is no announcement of "Game, set, and match" from the chair. The crowd waits. Everyone is puzzled, stunned. Navratilova approaches the chair. "The ball was out, right?" she asks. The umpire nods yes. Still no announcement. Martina turns to the chair again and prompts, "That's the match, right?" Again he nods yes. The crowd bristles. And the chair umpire remains silent.

Such a great match should never have ended on such a strange, inconclusive note. The crowd felt cheated because they didn't think the drama was rightfully over. Evert felt cheated because she thought the ball was good, and the score now deuce. Navratilova felt cheated because she could not fully enjoy her victory.

So what went wrong? What should have happened? Many felt Navratilova should have insisted the point be replayed. But Martina was not certain if the ball was in or out. She looked immediately to the one person who was officially designated to make the call and he saw the ball out. Should Martina overrule the linesman if she was uncertain herself?

What about an overrule by the chair umpire if he had a question about the call? An overrule on match point from the opposite side of the court on a ball "too close to call" would be unforgivable. Just ask Tom Gullikson about Joyce Johnson's overrule on match point at the 1986 U.S. Open.

In my mind, the chair umpire had only one option—make certain the linesman actually called the ball out and, if so, announce "Game, set, and match."

How different would the situation have been in the Martina-Chris match had there been no linesman? Most of us play our matches without the benefit of an objective third party on the line. In Navratilova's case, without a linesman, she would have had to call the ball good because any doubt must be ruled in favor of one's opponent. Rather than the match being over, the score would have been deuce, and perhaps an entirely different ending might have followed.

Line-calling is a major source of pressure and frustration for most players. With fractions of inches separating "in" from "out," with balls traveling at speeds in excess of 100 miles per hour, and with players running, jumping, and sprinting in every direction as they strain to see the line, it's no wonder mistakes are made. Trained, totally objective, professional linesmen with their eyes glued to the line and bodies motionless aren't even perfect—far from it. Bad calls are an inevitable fact of life in tennis. They come in all shapes and sizes and generally occur at the most inopportune times. Some are intentional, some unintentional. But if you can't stand bad calls, you're in the wrong sport.

Like it or not, that's the way the game is played. The real issue for players is how to deal with bad calls so they don't end up costing them the match.

A typical bad-call scenario goes something like this: On the first bad call, you let it pass but give your opponent a look. On the second bad call, you challenge the call. You feel you must defend yourself by saying something like, "No way—that ball was good!" or "You can't call that ball out—it was clearly good." Your assumption is that you must fight for your rights and let your opponent know he can't cheat you and get away with it.

The conflict escalates from this point. By questioning your opponent's call, you've challenged his integrity. And that means *war!* Now he gets defensive and unreasonable. And there's no way he will reverse the call because he would essentially be admitting guilt. In addition, he's likely to start calling every close ball out.

Now you become furious. Convinced you're being cheated out of every close call, you lose your temper and go wild. You're so off balance emotionally that you can't play. You may end up losing to a vastly inferior player, and leave the court feeling frustrated and victimized.

Once you challenge your opponent's integrity, your only hope is to secure a linesman early in the match. But all too often none is available.

Here's my formula for handling bad calls. It's very important that you have a specific strategy planned well in advance of your match if you are to be successful.

- Before the match, determine whether linesmen are available should one be requested during play.

- Assume that most calls are made correctly and any mistakes by your opponent are made honestly.

- Never challenge the integrity of your opponent by directly or indirectly accusing him of cheating.
- If you continue to get what you consider to be bad calls, express your concern in one of the following ways:
    1. Ask for a linesman by politely saying you would like to get some help with line-calling.
    2. On what you consider to be a very bad call, simply ask for a clarification. In a nonthreatening tone of voice, say, "Are you sure?" or "Was that ball good?" Give your opponent a chance to revise his call without challenging his integrity. Always give your opponent a way out to save face.
    3. On bad calls, assume either your judgment was wrong or your opponent made an unintentional mistake.
- If you are convinced you're being cheated and no linesman is available, dig in and get challenged. Learn to become one of those players who plays better and gets more determined when he thinks his opponent is cheating him. He doesn't make excuses or complain. He simply refuses to lose to someone he thinks is deliberately making bad calls.

My experience with players has shown repeatedly that if you treat your opponent with respect and dignity, you'll get better calls in the long run. You're also likely to stay in better control emotionally. The general rule of thumb is to assume your opponents are honest, and they will tend to be more honest. In most cases, match results will be influenced more by your emotional response to bad calls than by the calls themselves. So don't be surprised when you get a bad call, and don't go crazy when it happens.

Brushing Off Bedlam

If you ever want to put your between-point rituals to the ultimate test, try to re-create a Davis Cup tie scenario, if you can. Millions of Americans watched the U.S. Davis Cup team lose its first-round tie in Paraguay in March 1987 and wondered what they would have done under the same circumstances.

"It's impossible to really comprehend how bad it was without being there," says Herb Krickstein, father of American Davis Cupper Aaron Krickstein. "TV could never capture the scope of what happened. It was absolutely unbelievable."

What would you have done if stones and bottle caps rained down on

Striking the right balance of competitiveness and fun is critical for Andre Agassi.

you as you turned to change sides; degrading obscenities—racial and religious—were screamed at you; drums pounded after almost every point; balls anywhere close to the line were called out; spectators hanging over bleachers spat on you as you were forced deep for a ball?

This is Davis Cup, perhaps the most important tournament in a player's career. Your country is depending on you, cameras are rolling, the crowd is going wild, the world is watching, and your opponent is playing out of his mind. It can't be real, but it is real. It's not a dream. It's your serve, a bottle cap just bounced off your racket, the linesman is laughing, and a voice behind you screams, "Gag, Yankee, gag!" as you start the point.

What would you have done? The American players succumbed to Paraguay and the elements 3-2, but Jimmy Arias, Aaron Krickstein, Ken Flach, Robert Seguso, and team captain Tom Gorman deserve credit for their mental control under extremely difficult conditions.

The lessons to be learned from the Paraguay experience can be applied to every player's game—even at the club level. Here are just a few:

When your big weapon goes, what should you do?

Against Hugo Chapacu, Arias lost his big gun—the forehand. It just wasn't there. His response was to play defensively, keep lots of balls in play. The strategy worked for a while, but when he tried to play aggressively again, to go for the big forehand when he needed to, it failed him. If you're a big hitter, stay with it. Drop the speed somewhat, play higher percentage shots, but play aggressively. If you're a hitter, hit it! Once you start pushing the ball, you've changed your basic playing style and it's likely to be very tough for you to find the big gun for the remainder of the match. More important, your fight and spirit will be diminished. Arias is a streetfighter, not a pusher. Becoming too defensive dampened the fire that, ultimately, was his best weapon.

When your opponent zones against you, what should you do?

Victor Pecci was brilliant against Krickstein in the decisive match; he played perhaps the match of his life. When your opponent "trees," hang in there, just as Krickstein did. Don't get intimidated. Don't try to change your basic style and start going for unbelievable shots. Stay within yourself and be ready when your opponent returns to earth again. Unfortunately for Krickstein, Pecci never did.

How do you handle the pressure of big points in doubles?

The first and most important thing is not to allow anything to break or weaken the connection between you and your partner. Handle the pressure together as a team. Mutual support and team spirit are the answers to pressure situations in doubles. When you allow the pressure to come between you and your partner, the battle is lost.

How do you keep from losing your cool if you are cheated or ridiculed?

No adversity can *force* you to abandon your personal ethics, your standards of sportsmanship, and your sense of pride in who or what you are. The dictum still goes—"No Excuses!"

How do you keep your concentration when distractions are everywhere?

The real reason airplane noise, lawn mowers, dogs barking, and people talking disrupt concentration is the effect we allow them to have on our emotions. We begin connecting these irritating events to our mistakes; they become convenient excuses. As a result, we get increasingly more upset, disgusted, and even furious. That's precisely when our concentration comes apart. One of the best ways to keep the positive emotion and concentration flowing is to simply start saying, "I love it, I love it" to yourself. The more you love it, the less distracting the disruptions will be.

How do you prepare for a match that you are clearly expected to win, though in your eyes your opponent is very tough and difficult to play?

If our Davis Cup team had won, little would have been said because we were supposed to win. Paraguay was the classic no-win confrontation.

The first step in preparing for a no-win match is to realize what you're up against. Be prepared mentally when your opponent starts making unbelievable shots, maybe even zoning at times. If you expect it, you're not likely to become upset or discouraged. If you don't panic and get negative, you'll be ready to seize the opportunity when your opponent returns to his normal level of play. Rarely does your opponent's exceptional play last for an entire match, unless he senses your discouragement or frustration. Be prepared to be more nervous and tentative than normal. Resist playing defensive, safe tennis. Stay with the style of play you're accustomed to under normal conditions, even if you make errors.

Stay with the game plan you know will work best and eventually the balls will start landing in the court. It's important to keep in mind that you're under great pressure, and he very little, and that evens things out considerably. Your edge will be to stay strong emotionally and concentrate to do your best on every point. Because you don't want to lose to someone weaker than you, excuses, tanking, and anger become very seductive traps. Victory will be yours if you can keep your ego under control and perform emotionally.

When you're ahead 5-1 in a set, how do you keep from losing it?

At 5-1 or 5-2, your opponent has nothing to lose, so he often starts going for broke. The player who is down often starts playing more aggressively, loses his nervousness, and plays better. Players who are ahead tend to become nervous and start playing conservatively, trying not to lose. The combination often results in the lead player dropping the next game or two, maybe even the set. Two things are important here: First, never be surprised when your opponent hits a great shot or two at this time; expect it. The level of your opponent's game is likely to rise. Don't panic—it's only temporary. Second, resist strongly the temptation to play conservative tennis. Try to reverse things in your mind and play as if you're down 1-5. Keep playing the way you did to get ahead 5-1. Be aggressive.

Chapter VII

YOUR GOALS AND ATTITUDES: GETTING THE MOST OUT OF THE GAME

In the world of competitive tennis, there are many demons just aching to make the sport more difficult, complex, frustrating, and even frightening than it was ever meant to be. Poor playing conditions, injuries, nervousness, and stress all conspire to interfere with a player's enjoyment of the game.

To combat the demons, you need two things: the proper attitude and constructive goals. The proper attitude means remembering that tennis is a game—a recreational game that's best enjoyed by setting realistic, achievable goals, working to fulfill those goals with an enthusiastic spirit, and feeling rewarded by knowing that you've given it your all, have been a good sport, and benefited physically, mentally, and emotionally by the contest.

Tennis could be called a state of mind. And if you appreciate the fun, the great exercise, and the challenging test of your abilities; if you relish the fact that every day offers an opportunity to improve your skills, and every match is a chance to play your absolute, most glorious best—then you will brush aside the tennis demons and get a life's worth of satisfaction from the game.

A Model Student

If you wish that you could enjoy the game more, if you feel you don't get as much out of tennis as other people seem to, for whatever reason—a somewhat negative disposition, an intolerance of losing, a disdain for mediocrity—there's hope for you yet. Your attitude toward the sport can change. Andre Agassi's did.

There are many exciting qualities about Agassi, but the most significant and curious one is the dramatic emotional transformation that occurred in him in the two years before his rise to No. 3 in the world in 1988.

When I first arrived at the Nick Bollettieri Tennis Academy in 1985, I saw a spunky teenager who showed flashes of brilliance physically, but emotionally was a complete mixture of adjectives: driven, moody, angry, competitive, temperamental, edgy, nervous, and unpredictable. But, suddenly, Agassi has emerged as a player of unusual presence, poise, perspective, maturity, and control. In terms of emotional turnarounds, this has to be at the top of the list in my years of sports psychology. To suddenly balance his fight and competitiveness with such perspective, sportsmanship, humor, and positiveness is truly amazing.

Is it real? I think so. Agassi's thoughts on the matter are intriguing: "Up until 1986 I was competitive but could only accept winning. Winning was everything. If I wasn't winning, I couldn't handle it. I was very self-centered. I've come to understand that my problems on the court were really problems in me off-court."

Agassi points to two major forces that produced the emotional turnaround. The first was the revitalization of his Christian beliefs and the second was the unwavering confidence Bollettieri showed in him during the really tough times.

According to Agassi, his religious beliefs diminished the pressure to win, and Bollettieri kept him believing in himself until his talent finally surfaced.

"I had to go through some really bad times before I could start taking responsibility for myself," Agassi recalls. "Now I'm playing for myself and that's a big difference. Playing for someone else makes you very lonely. . . . Suddenly I realized I could still be competitive and say 'nice shot.' And it's not a facade . . . the thought of losing doesn't bother me now. It only bothers me if I haven't given 100-percent effort. So the pressure is off. If I lose, I lose. I now know that if I stay positive and keep on working, my talent will eventually come out."

I'm excited for Agassi. I'm excited about the impact he can have on young, developing players in this country. His on-court demeanor, pres-

The right chemistry between you and your partner is everything in doubles. Good communication is the key. Mark Woodforde and John McEnroe.

ence, sportsmanship, and mental toughness are fabulous models for others. The fact that he turned himself around is dramatic confirmation that one need not compromise sportsmanship and perspective to be competitive. Quite the contrary. When the balance was properly struck, Agassi's game suddenly became fun and with it came his magic.

Redefining Your Goals

Perhaps one of the most appealing things about tennis is its dynamic nature. The playing conditions, the opponents, even the player's own game, are always changing. The mental game also changes; in fact, it evolves. The beginner must be committed and have an enthusiastic attitude as he learns the strokes; the intermediate player starts to think about strategy and how to outsmart his opponent; the advanced player develops mental toughness.

Sometimes, however, the player's skills decline midway through his career. This doesn't mean the once elite competitor doesn't need mental toughness anymore; quite the opposite. This is when the player must graduate from "Standard Mental Toughness" to "Heavy-Duty Mental Toughness."

What's the difference? The standard variety is simply winning big points, big matches, big tournaments, never saying quit, loving craziness, diving for balls—all the usual stuff. Compared to Heavy-Duty Mental Toughness, however, it's a cakewalk. The heavy-duty variety is reserved for such special situations as wheelchair tennis, playing with real pain and injury, and kids playing under the impossible arm of overinvolved, overbearing, overzealous parents. Something else should be added to that list: it can be technically referred to as "The Withering Warrior Plight."

Here's the typical scenario. You've always been proud of your accomplishments in tennis. You played as a junior and always had a ranking. As a collegiate player you did well even against top schools. You even have had a national ranking at one time. You're no latecomer to the game. You paid your dues. In your mind, you're a *player*—and always have been. You're no *hack!* And you've got lots of dusty trophies to back up your claim. You're proud of the fact that your trademark as a junior and in college was that you were a super-tough competitor. Nobody beat you without a fight!

And today? Well, the fight is still there, but the rest of it—your eyes, your hands, your feet, your skills—they ain't the same. You're losing to guys who shouldn't even be on the same court with you. People who couldn't have gotten a game five years ago are nailing you. One guy, a real hack who has only played three-and-a-half years, took you to a tie-breaker yesterday. The guy plays two to three hours every day and eats, drinks, and sleeps tennis. Losing to him would have been the final straw.

And the most embarrassing part is that you both are the same age! You can't even blame it on age. He gets better every week, and you get worse. He's in great shape and plays every day, and you're in lousy shape and never practice. He's either taking lessons, hitting on the ball machine, running a marathon, or climbing Mount Everest. It's disgusting. You wonder what the heck he does for a living. As for you, you just don't have the time. Your business is totally consuming and, if you get to play a match a week, you consider yourself lucky. It isn't fair. All those years of playing don't mean a thing. You get no respect. God forbid, you're becoming a hack.

Your ego can't stand it. And the locker-room talk is that you're losing it. Though atypical of you in the past, you often show intense anger, temper, and unfriendliness during play now. Your wife threatened to divorce you just last weekend following a husband/wife mixed doubles tournament at your club. You made a complete jerk of yourself. Both a hack and a jerk: what is happening?

What's happening is that your ego is getting ripped. And that spells trouble for anyone. You've created a lethal combination for yourself—high expectation for success, a fiercely competitive ego, and *no time* to practice your tennis.

What to do is the question. In many ways, this scenario relates to all whose lives are too complex and unpredictable to play and practice regularly. Three choices emerge to resolve the conflict. The first is simply to chuck the whole thing—to quit the game entirely. If you quit, the problem goes away. It's tempting, but you've never thought of yourself as a quitter. Quitting is the ultimate tank. That just doesn't feel right, and besides, you need the exercise and like the social contacts in spite of the problems.

Your second choice is obvious: you simply make more time in your crazy schedule for tennis. You make it a real priority in your life and plan accordingly. You'll probably have to cut some attractive things somewhere else to make it happen, but if it's a high enough priority you'll do it. Let's be realistic, however. The reason your friend who has only played three-and-a-half years is so fired up about his tennis and willing to commit so much of his life to the game is that each year he reaches a higher level than he ever has before. You remember how exciting that was for you and how driven you became because of it. Now, though, it's very different. Unless you were to drop everything and give your total life to training, you could never be as good as you once were. And depending on your age and past skill, even if you did give 100 percent of your time, you might never achieve what you once did. Creating passion to break *new* barriers is very possible. Creating passion for mediocrity is a different matter altogether.

The third choice should appeal to your competitive instincts. It challenges you to dig as deep as you can and come up with something very special—Heavy-Duty Mental Toughness. If you can achieve it, you can continue to play without embarrassment or anguish. A *renewed* sense of enjoyment and satisfaction will return when you play, and the raging warrior, hungry for another victory, will be silenced.

Here are the steps:

1   Spend time redefining the meaning of tennis in your life. Work to get a new perspective on the nature of the conflict you've been facing and your conscious decision to find a real solution. Success on the court will no longer be defined in terms of winning or losing or even playing well.

2   Make a list of new tennis goals and place them where you will see them daily:

   ■ to use tennis to exercise and become fitter;
   ■ to use tennis to make new friends and enjoy old ones;
   ■ to use tennis as a stress breaker not a stress maker;
   ■ to have fun and enjoy yourself through the medium of tennis.

3   Think of your tennis philosophy this way: I no longer must win or play well to feel good about myself. My self-esteem is no longer tied to winning, but rather my ability to adhere to my new tennis goals.

4   Understand that what you are asking of yourself requires much greater mental toughness than what you were able to muster as a player. To play, to compete, even to lose, with grace, enjoyment, and dignity is the ultimate test for the old warrior. And the reward is simply knowing that you have joined a super-elite corps.

Improving Your Doubles Chemistry

A player's good attitude, while important in singles, is absolutely vital in doubles. If one member of a doubles team becomes negative or loses emotional control, both will generally fall. To achieve your competitive potential in doubles, you must learn how to trigger the right chemistry between you and your partner. Ask any top player what's the most critical factor in determining a great doubles team and you're likely to get the same response: the chemistry between the two players. Talent, quickness, aggressiveness, and style are important, but, if the right chemistry isn't there, that special sparkle of greatness will never materialize. You've seen that sparkle with teams like Newcombe and Roche, Gottfried and Ramirez, King and Casals, McEnroe and Fleming, Navratilova and Shriver. They were exceptional because something special happened between each doubles team. Fans can sense it—a feeling of harmony and connection. The electricity of the team brings out the best from each individual and literally carries the team against tough opposition.

Even so, players rarely pay much attention to how doubles chemistry happens or why. Most assume it's a natural thing. You play with someone and, if it clicks, great. If it doesn't, you simply move on to another partner.

But is it possible for two players to develop the right chemistry? Can a husband and wife, mother and daughter, brother and sister do anything to improve their chances of becoming an effective doubles team?

Tim and Tom Gullikson elected not to play doubles together in 1981. Both wanted to, but . . . "We were too argumentative, too negative with each other," says Tom. "My singles game was poor and it carried over into my doubles. There wasn't a good feeling. There was no team spirit."

A year later, Tom and Tim became the No. 3–ranked doubles team in the world and repeated that ranking in 1983. From nowhere to third in the world, from not being able to play together to loving it; how did it happen?

"Tom was more supportive of me," explains Tim. "He was more energetic and enthusiastic. I could feel he was giving 100 percent all the time and that made me work harder. We had a much better feeling between us. We seemed to understand and appreciate each other more. In one sense, good doubles play is like a good marriage. It's really based on many of the same principles: mutual respect, trust, understanding, acceptance."

"The most important factor of all is solid communication," says Tom. "When Tim and I are communicating well and remain enthusiastically supportive of one another, that's when we're very tough to beat."

So what did the Gulliksons do to create the right chemistry between them? First, they made a commitment to give it another try even though each was doing well with other partners. Second, they started devoting time to practicing their doubles play, something they'd never done before. "The focus of our training had always been singles," says Tom. "Doubles was an afterthought. We made playing together important. We worked on everything: volleys, patterns, style, and strategy. We worked better as a team because we were better prepared."

They also committed themselves to being more supportive of each other. As Tom puts it, "Tim had a tendency to get too analytical and technical when he didn't play well and that often made things worse. I would give him a simple cue like 'take it on the rise' or 'hit it early' and it often helped. It kept him from analyzing too much."

Tom also tried to pump Tim up when he got down on himself. "Understanding our roles also helped," says Tim. "I'm a percentage player and he's a shotmaker. Shotmakers can run hot and cold. I took the pressure off Tom so he wouldn't be afraid to go for big shots on big points. When he'd miss the return on ad point I'd say, 'I'll get you another one,' and in that way let him know it was OK."

The standard definition of a good doubles player rarely includes any reference to emotional or communication skills, yet these are critical to successful play. From an emotional perspective, a good doubles player is one who helps his partner achieve his ideal performance state during play. This partner skillfully keeps him feeling calm and confident. His connection to his partner is supportive, encouraging, friendly, and even at times inspiring. It is never critical, pessimistic, or argumentative. A good doubles player is one who reads his partner well and is capable of effectively communicating back to the partner the kinds of messages, both verbal and nonverbal, that enhance their performance. Communicating the right messages to one's partner demands a basic understanding of that partner.

Below are some "attitude" pointers to help keep the positive emotion flowing and the chemistry on track between you and your partner during play.

- When your partner loses a critical point, compliment the opponent for a good shot.

- Show high energy, enthusiasm, and determination during tough times, particularly when your partner is struggling.

- Be careful what you're telling your partner with your body language. Nonverbal communication is often more powerful than verbal.

- When your partner is playing poorly, never allow yourself to start reducing your efforts. Now's the time to be inspirational.

- Treat your partner the way you'd like to be treated at all times.

- Use the word "we" a lot and *mean it!*

- Never take your frustration out on your partner—*never.*

- Figure out a way to keep your partner having fun. Smile, crack a joke, keep it light.

- Treat your partner with respect and dignity. Deal with problems when the match is over.

But if problems persist, what should I do?

If there's someone you really want to play doubles with, but it never seems to work, try again! Invariably, this someone is a family member— a spouse, parent, brother, or sister. It's important to understand that family combinations are frequently the most difficult type of doubles matchup. We all tend to be more sensitive with those we are closest to. A casual comment can suddenly become very personal. And subtle, seemingly insignificant gestures often become magnified, triggering negative emotions and insecurities. We also tend to be less patient and more critical of those close to us.

Combined, this translates into tough times for family partners unless they make a conscious effort to work together. Follow the three steps below:

1 Commit to try again. Commit to doing whatever is necessary to make things work.

2 Set aside valuable practice time to work on your doubles play with each other. Rehearse tactics, strategy, responsibilities, shot selection, and timing. The more you rehearse, the better your chances of playing well together, both physically and emotionally.

3 Commit yourself to doing whatever you can to help your partner achieve his ideal performance state during play. Communicate your likes and dislikes openly with him before and after play, and set clear goals to overcome obstacles.

Sustaining the Camp Spirit

For many people, the words *camp* and *fun* are synonymous; going to summer camp as a kid was always the highlight of the year. Roasting marshmallows, chasing squirrels, shuddering to ghost stories, making friends, and plenty of hysterical laughter were all courses in the standard curriculum. The camp experience was something to look forward to all year.

As a tennis player, if you carry this same sense of fun and enthusiasm into your tennis camp experience, you'll not only enjoy it more, but you'll learn at a much faster rate as well. Here are some suggestions to get the most out of your camp experience:

■ Create a complete "play frame" around the time period. Make up your mind that no matter what happens, you are going to have a great time and enjoy yourself. This will be your number-one objective.

■ Come to the camp with an open, flexible, nondefensive attitude. You'll likely be exposed to new and different ideas and ways of doing things. Now is not the time to be a super-critical thinker. Get into the flow of things and give everything a try. If you can enter the camp with your ego under control and your emotional computer cleared, your rate of learning and fun will likely be substantially accelerated.

■ Have a very patient attitude with yourself and others. Because of the newness of your environment, your initial level of play may be below par. New surroundings, new people, different altitude, humidity, and court surface all translate into a lower level of play at the beginning. Be patient.

■ Pace yourself physically and emotionally. This is probably more tennis than you've played since last year's camp. Blisters, sore feet, sunburn, and injuries can ruin a camp experience. Whenever possible, prepare yourself for camp by playing more, getting in shape, and conditioning your body and mind before you arrive. If that's not possible, start slowly and intelligently and, by mid-week, you'll still be in the camp blasting balls—not sidelined and frustrated.

■ Don't go to camp to prove anything. Entering camp with the attitude—"Once and for all I'm going to show these people I am a real player"—will simply leave you frustrated and disappointed. Camps are not designed to have you playing great when you walk in. Camps are for learning and conditioning; if you want to prove yourself, enter a tournament.

■ Make friends, not enemies, with people in your group. If you get overly competitive, don't be surprised if you eat alone in the evening. Remember, this is not a tournament environment, and the other players are not your opponents. Try to subdue that competitive drive and you'll make more friends, be less defensive, become more open to new ideas, and learn faster.

What to do when you leave. Most people get pretty excited when they think about how good they would get if they could keep the same rate of learning going for more than the week or two of camp. Comments like, "I really started playing great by the end of camp, but once I returned home, everything I learned started to fade," are common. The real key is to understand why the camp experience nearly always gets such positive results. Once you understand the reasons, you can take advantage of this accelerated learning all year. Here's what camp offers you:

- You hit more balls than any other time all year long. If you play more, you're going to get better faster. Make a commitment to spend more time on your tennis and hit more balls when you return home.

- Camp forces you to work on your weaknesses. Most people like to play rather than drill and so that's what they do—until they attend camp and are forced to drill. Set aside a certain percentage of your time each week for drilling on your weaknesses, either with a ball machine or a friend.

- Camp forces you to work harder than normal. You aren't allowed to get lazy and socialize on the court in most camps. Adopt the same attitude at home. Practice and play with the same intensity you do in camp and your rate of learning will reflect it.

- Camp forces you to be organized all week. Much planning and fore-thought went into designing your training time for the week. Start organizing your tennis time at home with the same thoughtfulness.

- The camp attitude keeps you feeling enthusiastic, highly motivated, and eager. Perhaps more than any other factor, your accelerated camp learning stems from this kind of emotional climate. Work on your attitude, set new and exciting goals for yourself, and make a commitment to generate more enthusiasm and fun in your tennis at home. You actually have much more control in this area than you may think. You don't have to wait until next year's camp to get the fires going.

If you want to continue the camp rate of learning on a year-round basis, or if, for whatever reason, you couldn't get to your favorite camp this year, there's still hope. You can create many of the same conditions at home that bring the super results at camp. Home will never be the same as camp, but much of the camp experience can be taken home. Be a year-round camper and watch your tennis game blossom.

The Big Picture

Players often write, asking me what you might call "big picture" questions about their games. We can often trace their long-term achievements and problems back to a positive or negative attitude, productive or counterproductive goals. Here are some of their letters:

> *Q I've had the opportunity to coach basketball, baseball, football, and tennis for 15 years. Why is it that the most talented athletes invari-*

*ably are the weakest mentally? What is it that causes the gifted ath-
letes to emotionally lag behind their peers? So often they are the
real "head cases." Do you agree?*

A I do. My experience with highly gifted athletes has been very similar. Gifted athletes learn the physical skills of their sport much
more easily than less talented peers. They don't have to try as hard,
work as hard, or produce the same effort to get the same result.
Consequently, they develop a poor work ethic.

In the early years, talented athletes are often successful even
though they have poor concentration, poor intensity, and a poor
attitude. Their superior natural ability carries them. And, because
they are able to perform better than their peers, the undesirable
habits get reinforced. Athletes who have little talent must concentrate harder, give superior effort, and maintain excellent emotional
control or they can't keep up. Poorer athletes are, therefore, rarely
"head cases," because they can't afford to be. The patterns of behavior are different for the talented athletes because the schedule
of success and reinforcement is different.

Another contributing factor is risk. Gifted athletes are reminded
of their talent constantly by coaches and parents. The label can actually become a burden. The athlete becomes afraid to give 100
percent, to put himself totally on the line for fear he or she won't
live up to everyone's expectations. "Maybe I'm not as great as they
think I am," the gifted athlete thinks. By being a head case, no one
will know if he really has the talent. He plays it safe, and protects
his self-esteem.

The key to working with talented athletes is to help them understand these pitfalls. The talent is both a gift and a burden. Successful
coaching and parenting of these kids require special understanding
or the "Head Case Syndrome" is likely to emerge.

Q *My daughter is 10 years old; all she wants to do is play tennis. She
would play 10 hours a day if I let her. We live within walking distance of our tennis club and she always wants to go and hang out.
Is it bad to let her play as much as she likes?*

A Yes it is. The child should always leave the court wanting to play
more. Early on, a child can get hooked on tennis, always wanting
more. Limiting time on the court reinforces the sense that tennis is
an opportunity, something to look forward to. It keeps the youngster eager.

If you allow a youngster to play all she wants, her interest level
will wane and her play will become sloppy. Her skills will not develop as quickly, and poor habits will set in because she's tired. The

Keeping a clear perspective is no easy task in big-time junior tennis. Chris Garner learned the hard way.

gym-rat syndrome—hanging out all day at the tennis club—is also to be avoided. One day a week at the club, perhaps a Saturday, won't hurt. But to live at the club for an entire summer or hang out at the club for three or four hours after school each day is not an effective strategy for sustaining high motivation and achievement. The specialness of playing has to be reinforced.

Q *Please help my mixed doubles partner and me resolve an ongoing dispute. My partner always says "nice shot" to his opponents after they win a point and it drives me crazy. He knows it bothers me but he can't seem to stop. I contend that he shouldn't be building up our opponents' confidence by saying "nice shot" all the time. He maintains that it's good sportsmanship and is just an old habit that certainly doesn't do anyone any harm.*

From a psychological perspective, should a player be saying "nice shot" whenever his opponents play a good point?

A Obviously, one should not say "nice shot" to build up the confidence of your opponent. However, there are justifiable reasons for occasionally saying it. The first is sportsmanship. When good sportsmanship becomes the highest competitive priority for players, everyone benefits. Tennis literally becomes a powerful teacher of life skills for young players. Emotional control, integrity, and maturity are natural by-products. For adults, when sportsmanship is emphasized, players report more fun, better play, and less stress.

Also, players who have temper problems and tend to get down on themselves find that verbally acknowledging an opponent's good shot often helps take the pressure off. They think, "I didn't screw up—they hit a great shot." The point is, if saying it helps you stay more positive, by all means say it. But players who constantly say "nice shot" out of insecurity or as a vehicle for socializing on the tennis court should reconsider this habit. In your case, the major issue is the impact of your partner's saying "nice shot" on you. The impact appears to be quite negative. The only solution is to have a thorough discussion with your partner and work out an agreement for the future. If your partner chooses not to stop, you must change your emotional response to him saying it, or the team will suffer. Good communication is the only answer to solving this one.

Q *I have been playing tennis for six years and have had some lessons. I play four to eight hours a day, six days a week, and now my game seems to be at a standstill. I'm not improving at all. I'm 18 and my friends think I should give up the idea of turning pro and just play for the fun of it. However, I am too much into it to forget about* *professional tennis. What can I do to improve my game? Are the odds against me becoming a professional player?*

A The tennis explosion throughout the world has vastly increased the difficulty of young players becoming Top Ten players. Realistically, the odds are very small that any player will achieve professional success at the highest level. If everything is right—you started early, have great coaching, a powerful game, and the right body type, and you're the No. 1 or 2 player in the country—the situation is still uncertain.

From the sound of your letter, you are not nationally ranked and have not been involved in competition at the highest level. It is always important to have dreams, but I would recommend you not define success solely in terms of professional play. I try to get players to view tennis as an important life experience that can teach them a variety of life skills.

It would be great if you became a pro, but that should not be the only reason you want to play well. I suspect that the pressure you're putting on yourself to reach the professional level is largely responsible for your recent lack of progress. Take the pressure off and focus on enjoyment and hard work. I think you'll find that, regardless of what happens in the long run, your tennis will be a valuable life experience.

Keeping a Clear Perspective

The negatives in the mental game of tennis can be tremendously destructive, but there's one sure-fire way to protect yourself from their effects— keep your perspective on *the game*. This is a lesson that's invaluable for all players, and can be especially useful if learned early in one's career, before a player has to go through any tough times. Former top-rated junior Chris Garner is an example of someone who learned about the importance of perspective a little too late. Garner was in a quandary.

"I felt like I was all alone. It seemed like I was fighting for my life. The pressure was unbelievable. People started to doubt me. My friends drifted away. Everyone was my friend when I was doing well, but when I started doing badly, I was alone.

"I've always wanted people to like me. I wanted to be accepted. I did everything I could to meet the expectations, but I couldn't. I totally lost perspective. I either made it in tennis or that was it. There was no life beyond tennis.

"I started working harder than ever on the court, but I stopped improving. Every time I lost it was a killer. I had to win and couldn't. I walked on the court with the match and walked off the court with the match. Everywhere I went all I could see was tennis. I was very unhappy. I became cynical and distant. I felt deserted, I stopped believing in myself, and I stopped trusting others."

So recalled Garner in reliving the two miserable years that he's now put behind him. "College broke the negative cycle," said Garner, who walked away an All-American in 1988 when he completed his freshman year at the University of Georgia. "It was a lifesaver. Being part of a team helped me find myself again. The guys on the team were great. We became friends. It didn't matter whether you were No. 1 or No. 6; everyone was equally important in terms of his contribution to a successful team effort. I love the game again, and it's great. I can look back and see it all very clearly now. It's so easy to lose perspective."

Garner's junior life was full of fairy tales. He was ranked No. 2 his second year in the national 12s and No. 5 his first year of the 14s. In 1984, at 14, he left his home in Bayshore, New York, and became a full-time student at the Nick Bollettieri Tennis Academy, where he thrived in the intense academy lifestyle. He made it to No. 1 in the second year of the 14s and his first year of the 16s. At 15, Garner was ready to turn pro. He had an all-court game, was exceptionally talented, and was tough as nails mentally. And coming from a home with limited means had filled him with a hunger to succeed. "I'd rather be poor and become rich because I have the drive. I want it more and work harder than the other guys," he said.

But Garner's career began to hit a downward spiral with a loss to Glenn Layendecker in the final round of qualifying at the 1985 Lipton International Players Championships. "In my mind I was ready to turn pro, and had I won that match I'm sure I would have," Garner said. "Instead, I had to go back and play the juniors and mentally I had already moved on. I didn't want to play the juniors anymore, and when I had to, the pressure really got to me. I had worked harder than anyone. I felt my game was ready and mentally I was sure I could make it. I was the top seed in just about every tournament, but I didn't win another junior event for two years."

What happened to Garner isn't so unusual, particularly at the apex of junior tennis. The real issue is perspective. The time, the money, the pressure, the expectations, the sacrifices, and the fame make it easy to lose perspective. It's a constant battle for players, coaches, and parents to maintain a clear vision of what it all means. The right perspective reduces pressure, fear of failure, and threat to self-esteem. It increases the sense of enjoyment and leads to a deeper sense of self-motivation and involvement. Most importantly, it builds the foundation for healthy personal development.

Here is what I consider the right perspective in tennis:

Tennis is not bigger than life, nor is it life itself. It's never a life-and-death issue; there is always life after tennis. Tennis is not about making it—being ranked No. 1, reaching the Top Ten, being selected for the national team, or turning pro. Tennis is about who you are and what you become inside. Self-worth is never measured in terms of winning and losing. Tennis is a life experience, one that should make you better as a person. The real issue is not winning trophies, titles, or national championships, but what's happening as a result of tennis: do you feel better about yourself, about who you are, what you're becoming, and where you're going?

Tennis is a powerful teacher. The struggle to achieve, to extend beyond normal limits, to reach new levels of personal competency and skill, and to conquer your innermost fears and doubts is what life is all about and what tennis is all about. The struggle should make you stronger, not weaker, as a person. Tennis should increase your range of personal competency because of the life skills it involves. There is never one tournament, one match, or one point that will make or break you. Tennis is much bigger than that. The right perspective in tennis is the big picture, and the big picture is *you*.

Tennis should be played because it's a great sport and because it's good for you. The time, money, and sacrifices it entails must be justified on this basis. And if you become a great player along the way, that's icing on the cake. Making it big isn't the critical issue. What *is* critical is maintaining the right perspective. Regardless of where you end up on the computer, the payoff will be worth the price.